I Step From
A Famous Story

Adapted as Dramatic Readings

by Clay Franklin

A Samuel French Acting Edition

SAMUEL FRENCH
FOUNDED 1830

New York Hollywood London Toronto

SAMUELFRENCH.COM

Copyright © 1965 by Samuel French, Inc.

ALL RIGHTS RESERVED

CAUTION: Amateurs may produce the material in this book without payment of a Licensing Fee. Professionals are hereby warned that *I STEP FROM A FAMOUS STORY* is subject to a Licensing Fee. It is fully protected under the copyright laws of the United States of America, the British Commonwealth, including Canada, and all other countries of the Copyright Union. All rights, including professional, motion picture, recitation, lecturing, public reading, radio broadcasting, television and the rights of translation into foreign languages are strictly reserved. In its present form the play is dedicated to the reading public only.

Stock licensing fees quoted upon application to Samuel French, Inc.

For all other rights than those stipulated above, apply to: Samuel French, Inc.

Particular emphasis is laid on the question of professional readings, permission and terms for which must be secured in writing from Samuel French, Inc.

Copying from this book in whole or in part is strictly forbidden by law, and the right of performance is not transferable.

Whenever the play is produced the following notice must appear on all programs, printing and advertising for the play: "Produced by special arrangement with Samuel French, Inc."

Due authorship credit must be given on all programs, printing and advertising for the play.

No one shall commit or authorize any act or omission by which the copyright of, or the right to copyright, this play may be impaired.
No one shall make any changes in this play for the purpose of production.
Publication of this play does not imply availability for performance. Both amateurs and professionals considering a production are strongly advised in their own interests to apply to Samuel French, Inc., for written permission before starting rehearsals, advertising, or booking a theatre.
No part of this book may be reproduced, stored in a retrieval system, or transmitted in any form, by any means, now known or yet to be invented, including mechanical, electronic, photocopying, recording, videotaping, or otherwise, without the prior written permission of the publisher.

ISBN 978-0-573-60067-8   Printed in U.S.A.   #11907

Grateful Acknowledgments: Adaptation of *Mrs. McWilliams and the Lightning* from *The American Claimant* by Mark Twain. Reprinted with the permission of Harper & Row, Publishers, Incorporated.

Permission for *The Idyl of Red Gulch* by Bret Harte, by Houghton Mifflin Co.

The Society of Authors as the literary representative of the Estate of the late W. W. Jacobs for permission to include *The Monkey's Paw*.

"They are a most useful anthology and come off remarkably well. The publication of this book fills a definite need."

Margaret Webster

INTRODUCTION

The following well-known tales are given a new look by having the main character from each tell the story. Such a treatment should prove entertaining when read aloud, whether it be before an audience in the classroom, from a platform, or at ease in an armchair.

For those who have the urge to display their dramatic talents, a number of them can be memorized and acted out in the usual monologue fashion.

If the reader is not acquainted with some of the authors here represented, these samples may whet the literary appetite so that more of their stories will be read.

Whenever possible the actual dialogue of the author has been retained. However, in some instances, to sustain the story line or add a dramatic finish, additional dialogue had to be supplied. In those cases every effort was made to capture the mood and style of the original author. An attempt has been made to arrange them in chronological order.

In presenting these fictional characters, it is suggested that the reader become familiar with the material beforehand, so that frequent glances can be directed to your audience. That will assure more listening interest. Then too, there is an opportunity to impersonate by vocal interpretation.

And now let's open the pages so these imaginary people can step forth and relive their stories.

CONTENTS

MOTHER RIGBY 1
    From *Feathertop: A Moralized Legend* by Nathaniel Hawthorne

DR. HEIDEGER 8
    From *Dr. Heideger's Experiment* by Nathaniel Hawthorne

MRS. LIRRIPER 16
    From *Mrs. Lirriper's Lodgings* by Charles Dickens

PEASANT 21
    From *What the Old Man Does Is Always Right* by Hans Christian Andersen

MR. THOMAS 27
    From *The Tell-Tale Heart* by Edgar Allan Poe

THE MARQUISE DE R—— 32
    From *The Marquise* by George Sand

MR. MARKHEIM 42
    From *Markheim* by Robert Louis Stevenson

MISS MARY 50
    From *The Idyl of Red Gulch* by Bret Harte

DORIAN GRAY 57
    From *The Picture of Dorian Gray* by Oscar Wilde

Contents

MADAME LOISEL 68
From *The Diamond Necklace* by Guy de Maupassant

MR. WHITE 74
From *The Monkey's Paw* by W. W. Jacobs

MRS. MCWILLIAMS 83
From *Mrs. McWilliams and the Lightning* by Mark Twain

"DOC" SILVERTON 90
From *To Make a Hoosier Holiday* by George Ade

MISS CANDACE WHITCOMB 99
From *The Village Singer* by Mary E. Wilkins Freeman

PERKINS OF PORTLAND 106
From *The Adventure of the Crimson Cord* by Ellis Parker Butler

MADAME KOLPAKOW 112
From *The Chorus Girl* by Anton Chekov

RANSIE BILBRO 117
From *The Whirligig of Life* by O. Henry

DELLA YOUNG 122
From *The Gift of the Magi* by O. Henry

MOTHER RIGBY

From *Feathertop: A Moralized Legend*

One of America's greatest writers, Nathaniel Hawthorne, took many of his themes from his rich New England heritage.
This nineteenth century tale is spiced with black magic, humor, and worldly truth. The protagonist is Mother Rigby, an old witch. Perhaps that label is sufficient to describe her. She is hovering by her kitchen hearth and in a few minutes she will display some of her magical powers.

'Tis true. As everybody must have heard, I am a witch. I daresay I am one of the most potent witches in New England. If you wish proof of what I speak —behold. I smoke this pipe. But it is cold. I need a coal for it. So I say, "Dickon! A coal for my pipe."

There. See how the bowl glows—and how the smoke curls from my lips. Dickon is my invisible messenger. "Thank ye, Dickon!"

But to return to my task. I arose before sunrise to commence. I am making a scarecrow. Alas, the crows and blackbirds have already found the corn peeping up from the soil.

Now I don't want to set up a hobgoblin in my own corn patch. I could do it if I so pleased, but I'm tired of doing marvelous things. And there is no use scaring little children for a mile roundabout. No, the scarecrow shall be a gentleman.

Here I have a broomstick. On many a midnight I have galloped on this. But now it will be his spinal column. Next, his arms. This pudding stick will do for one—and a broken rung from a chair will be the other. I tie them loosely. As for his legs—here is a hoe handle—and a stick I found in the woodpile. I stuffed this meal bag with straw for his lungs, heart, and stomach. So there it is—a body with no head.

I found this withered and shrivelled pumpkin. I cut two holes for his eyes and a slit for his mouth—and a bluish-colored knob in the middle to pass for a nose. Don't laugh. I've seen worse heads on human shoulders. Many a fine gentleman has a pumpkin head.

Now he needs clothes. Here is a velvet waistcoat of ample size. Then a pair of silk stockings on those sticks for legs—and a pair of scarlet breeches. Then to pretend the poor puppet has feet, I tie on these shoes. I spied them on an ash heap while soaring by on my broomstick. The finest of all is this plum-colored coat. It was made in London and has embroidery on the cuffs, pocket-flaps, and buttonholes.

What matter if it has patches on the elbow. Such finery for a puppet.

His scalp looks bare. Here is a wig. It was worn by my dead husband. And on top of that this dusty three-cornered hat. The tail feather of a rooster is stuck in it.

There. Come, look at me. Ah! I've made many a puppet since I've been a witch, but methinks this is the finest of them all. 'Tis almost too good for a scarecrow.

Yes, this puppet is too good a piece of work to stand all summer in a corn patch. He's capable of better things. Why, I've danced with a worse one, when partners happened to be scarce, at our witch meetings in the forest. What if I should let him take his chance among other men of straw who are just as empty and go bustling about the world?

Well, I don't mean to dabble in witchcraft today, further than the lighting of my pipe. But as a witch I am, and a witch I'm likely to remain, I'll make a man of my scarecrow.

"Here, my fine fellow, take my pipe. Puff, darling, puff. Puff away, my precious. Your life depends on it. It is the breath of life to ye. Well done, my pretty one. Again. Puff out the very bottom of thy heart!

"But why lurkest thou in the corner, lazy one? Step forth! Thou hast the world before thee! Extend thy arm—thy leg. Take a step. Well done. Again.

"I am pleased. Thou hast a man's aspect. Now

thou shalt have the mockery of a voice. I bid thee speak! Do not gasp, my precious one, speak—like I am doing.

"There. Thou canst speak, darling. Thou called me Mother. But thou shalt say a thousand things and say them a thousand times over—like men do in the world.

"And now, darling, I have taken great pains with thee and thou art so beautiful, that I love thee better than any other witch's puppet in the world. And I've made them of all sorts—from clay, wax, straw sticks, night fog, and chimney smoke. But thou art the very best. So give heed to what I say.

"With all thy heart, sayest thou? I laugh. Thou hast such a pretty way of speaking. With all thy heart. And thou didst put thy hand to the left side of thy waistcoat as if thou really hadst one!

"But now, my pretty one, thou must go and play thy part in the great world. And thou canst hold up thy head with the best of them. Never fear, thou shalt have wealth—a gold mine in Eldorado—a castle in the air—and a chateau in Spain. But for ready money, here is a copper farthing.

"Oh, I have a clever plan, my darling. Over there in the city lives a merchant, Master Gookin. He hath a beautiful daughter, Polly. So hark ye, my lovely. Thou hast a fair outside and a pretty wit of thine own. Sigh, smile, flourish thy hat, thrust forth thy leg like a dancing master, and pretty Polly Gookin is thine own!

"Hold thou the pipe, my precious one, while I fill it for thee again.

"Dickon! Another coal for this pipe!

"There. See how the red spark of fire is glowing. Now hark to this: Whatever may happen to thee, thou must stick to thy pipe. Thy life is in it. Smoke, puff, blow clouds of it. Tell the people, if any questions be made, that it is for thy health, and that so the physician orders thee to do. And, sweet one, when thou shalt find thy pipe getting low, go apart into some corner and cry sharply, 'Dickon. A fresh pipe of tobacco!'—or 'Dickon, another coal for my pipe!' Then put it into thy pretty mouth as speedily as may be. Else, instead of a gallant gentleman in a gold-laced coat, thou will be but a jumble of sticks and tattered clothes, a bag of straw, and a withered pumpkin.

"Oh, thou speak with wisdom. Of course thou shalt thrive like an honest man. Here, take my staff with thee. There—with a wave of my hand it is now a cane with a gold head. That gold head has as much sense in it as thine own. It will guide thee straight to Master Gookin's door.

"Get thee gone, my pretty one. If any ask thy name, say it is Feathertop, for thou hast a feather in thy hat. Now depart, my treasure, and good luck go with thee!"

And Feathertop strode manfully toward the door. I watched him from the threshold, well pleased to see how the sunbeams glistened on him and how lovingly he smoked his pipe. Then I chanted a witch benediction after him as he disappeared down the road.

I did no sorcery for the rest of that day. Then twilight came. I was seated by the kitchen hearth and had just shaken the ashes out of a new pipe— when I heard a clatter outside. It did not seem like the tramp of a human but as the rattle of sticks or dry bones.

Ha! What step is that? Whose skeleton is out of the grave now, I wonder?

The door opened—and there was my Feathertop. He limped into the room.

"Feathertop! What has gone wrong? Did Master Gookin thrust my darling from his door? The villain! I'll set twenty fiends to torment him till he offers thee his daughter on his bended knee!

"It was not that? Did the girl scare my precious one? I'll cover her face with pimples. Her nose shall be as red as the coal in thy pipe! Her front teeth shall drop out! In a week hence she shall not be worth thy having!

"It was not so? Then what was it? Thou met Polly Gookin. Go on. Lord Feathertop they called thee. Wonderful. And then? Thou spoke pretty words with thy hand on thy heart. Well done, my precious. Go on. Ah, she glanced at thee with eyes of love and held thy hand. Thou acted truly like a gallant gentleman. What went wrong? Oh! She looked in a mirror

Mother Rigby

—and so did ye! Alas. Mirrors are a curse. Only human fools look in them. Then she screamed and fainted, sayest thou. And what didst thou behold in the mirror? Ah, poor puppet. Only thy patches, sticks, and a pumpkin head—instead of a man.

"Beware, Feathertop! Do not take thy pipe from thy mouth. Alas, thou flung it against the chimney. Thou threw away thy breath of life. There. Look at thee now. A heap of rags, and sticks, and a shrivelled pumpkin."

Poor fellow. There are thousands of coxcombs and charlatans in the world who are made up of just such a jumble of forgotten and good-for-nothing trash as he was. Yet they live in fair repute and never see themselves for what they are. Why should my poor puppet be the only one to know himself and perish for it?

Poor Feathertop. I could easily give him another chance and send him forth again tomorrow. But his feelings are too tender. He seems to have too much heart to bustle for his own advantage in such an empty and heartless world. So I will make a scarecrow of him after all. 'Tis an innocent and useful vocation and will suit my darling well.

There on the floor is his pipe of tobacco. I shall pick it up. I need it more than he.

"Dickon! Another coal for my pipe!"

DR. HEIDEGER

From *Dr. Heideger's Experiment*

Here is another tale of sorcery by Nathaniel Hawthorne.

The townspeople babbled many fantastic rumors about old Dr. Heideger and his strange powers. Imagine that he is conducting us to his study where an amazing experiment will take place.

Follow me into the room. It may appear dingy and old-fashioned to you. As you see, it is festooned with cobwebs and besprinkled with antique dust. The damask curtains are faded. Along the walls are several oaken bookcases. Over there is a mirror in a tarnished gilt frame. On that wall is a portrait of Miss Sylvia Ward, in her gown of satin and brocade. We were to be married, but alas, she died the evening before the ceremony. She had complained of being ill, so I prepared a potion for her. Unfortunately it had dire consequences. Over that bookcase you see a bronze bust of Hippocrates.

But perhaps you wonder what knowledge is contained in that large, black leather book. Silver clasps keep it sealed from prying eyes. The people of the town whisper about that book. They say it has magic powers. You shall hear more about it.

One afternoon last summer I had invited four venerable friends of mine to come here to my study. Three of them were gentlemen, all white-bearded—Mr. Medbourne, Colonel Killigrew, and Mr. Gascoigne—and a withered gentlewoman, Widow Wycherly. They were all old and melancholy creatures whose greatest misfortune was that they were not in their graves.

On that round table I had placed a cut-glass vase which was covered with a cloth, and four champagne glasses for my guests.

But allow me to mention a few words about each of my friends.

Mr. Medbourne had been a prosperous merchant but lost all by a frantic speculation.

Colonel Killigrew had wasted his best years, his health and substance in the pursuit of sinful pleasures. These gave birth to a brood of pains, such as the gout, and other torments of soul and body.

Mr. Gascoigne was a ruined politician—a man of evil fame—until time had made him obscure instead of infamous.

As for the Widow Wycherly, tradition tells us that she was a great beauty in her day, a long while past, and had lived in seclusion because of certain scandalous stories. It is worth mentioning too, that each of these three old gentlemen, Mr. Medbourne, Colonel Killigrew, and Mr. Gascoigne were early lovers of the Widow Wycherly, and had once been on the point of cutting each other's throats for her sake.

But to recall that afternoon when I expected my four friends.

After they arrived here, I motioned them to be seated.

"My dear old friends, I am desirous of your assistance in a little experiment."

Then I hobbled across the room, picked up the black book of magic, and returned to the table. I undid the silver clasp and took from its pages a rose. Rather, I should say, it was once a rose. The crimson petals and green leaves had turned to a brownish hue which seemed ready to crumble to dust in my hands.

"This rose," I said with a sigh, "this same withered and crumpling flower, blossomed five and fifty years ago. It was given me by Sylvia Ward, whose portrait hangs yonder. I meant to wear it on our wedding day. For all that time it has been treasured between the leaves of this old volume. Now, would you deem it possible that this rose of half a century could ever bloom again?"

Widow Wycherly said it was impossible. That I might as well ask whether an old woman's wrinkled face could ever bloom again.

"Watch!" I commanded.

Dr. Heideger

I uncovered the vase and threw the faded rose into the water which it contained. At first, it lay on the surface of the fluid. Soon, however, the crushed and dead petals stirred and became a deep crimson. The slender stalk became green again. It was as if the flower was revived from a deathlike slumber.

My friends were impressed. They called it a pretty deception and asked how it happened.

"Did you ever hear of the Fountain of Youth? Ponce de Leon searched for that centuries ago. He never sought it in the right place. This famous Fountain of Youth is situated in the southern part of the Floridian peninsula, near Lake Nacaco. There several gigantic magnolias have kept fresh as vio'ets through the centuries. An acquaintance of mine, knowing my curiosity in such matters, has sent me some of that magic water that you see in this vase."

Then they became curious how this fluid would affect the human frame.

"You shall judge for yourselves. All of you are welcome to as much of this admirable fluid as may restore the bloom of youth. For my part, having had much trouble in growing old, I am in no hurry to grow young again. With your permission, I will merely watch the progress of the experiment."

As I spoke, I filled the four champagne g'asses with the water of the Fountain of Youth. It bubb'ed, and they were eager to swallow it at once.

"Before you drink, my respectable old friends, you

should draw up a few rules. With the experience of a lifetime to direct you, be cautious in passing a second time through the perils of youth. Think what a shame it would be if with your peculiar advantages, you should not become patterns of virtue and wisdom to all the young people of the age."

They made no reply. One laughed feebly.

"Drink, then. I rejoice that I have so well selected the subjects of my experiment."

With palsied hands they raised the glasses to their lips. After they had consumed the liquid they returned the glasses on the table.

Almost immediately there was an improvement in the spirit of the party. A sudden glow of cheerful sunshine brightened their faces. There was a healthful color on their cheeks instead of the ashen hue. They gazed at each other and fancied that some magic power had really begun to smooth away the sad inscription which Father Time had engraved on their brows. The Widow Wycherly adjusted her cap and smiled saucily.

They wanted more of the wondrous water so they would become younger.

"Patience, patience," I said as I watched them. "You have been a long time growing old. Surely, you might be content to grow young in half an hour."

But they were eager for more, so again I filled their glasses.

Their eyes grew clear and bright. A dark shade deepened among their silvery locks. As they sat around the table they appeared as three gentlemen of middle years and a woman hardly beyond her buxom prime.

Colonel Killigrew looked longingly at the widow and remarked that she looked charming. She ran to the mirror and thrust her face close to the glass and observed the absence of long-remembered wrinkles. Pleased, she curtsied and simpered to her reflection.

As though the weight of years had been removed, the three gentlemen became exhilarated. Colonel Killigrew sang a jolly song while his eyes wandered toward the buxom figure of the Widow Wycherly. Mr. Gascoigne's mood seemed to run on political topics, as he proclaimed patriotism and the people's rights. Mr. Medbourne was involved with the calculation of dollars and cents. He spoke about a project for supplying ice to the East Indies by harnessing a team of whales to the polar icebergs.

The widow approached me with a sort of dancing step and asked for another drink.

"Certainly, my dear madam, certainly." And again I filled their glasses.

They were now in the happy prime of youth. Age, with its miserable train of cares and sorrows and diseases, was remembered only as a troubled dream from which they had joyously awoke. They laughed loudly at their old-fashioned attire. With mischievous merriment, the Widow Wycherly coaxed me to get up and dance with her.

"Pray excuse me. I am old and rheumatic and my dancing days were over long ago. But either of these gay young gentlemen will be glad of so pretty a partner."

Colonel Killigrew requested that she dance with him, but Mr. Gascoigne shouted that he would be her partner. Mr. Medbourne joined them and exclaimed that the widow had promised her hand to him fifty years ago.

They all gathered around her. One caught both her hands in a passionate embrace—another threw his arm about her waist—the third buried his hand among the glossy curls that clustered beneath the widow's cap. She blushed, panted, chided, and laughed as she strove to disengage herself. Never was there a livelier picture of youthful rivalship, with bewitching beauty for the prize.

Yet as I glanced in the mirror, it reflected three old, gray and withered men grappling for the attention of a shrivelled crone.

But they continued to struggle, grasping at one another's throats. In their combat about the room the table was overturned and the vase was dashed into a thousand fragments. The precious Water of Youth flowed in a bright stream across the floor.

"Come, come, gentlemen—come, Madam Wycherly. I really must protest against this riot!"

They stood still, as if listening to Time calling them back from their sunny youth. They became aware that their violent exertions had wearied them, and returned to their seats.

I held the rose in my hand. "My poor Sylvia's rose. It appears to be fading again."

And so it did. While we looked at it, the flower continued to shrivel up, till it became as dry and fragile as before.

My friends gazed at each other. Then they sadly asked me if they were old again.

"Yes, friends, ye are old again. Lo! the Water of Youth is all lavished on the ground. Well, I bemoan it not. Even if the fountain gushed at my very doorstep, I would not stoop to bathe my lips on it. No, even if its delirium would last for years instead of minutes. Such is the lesson ye have taught me."

But I am afraid it taught my friends no such lesson. As they departed I heard them speak about making a pilgrimage to Florida. There they would quaff from the Fountain of Youth morning, noon, and night.

Alas, what folly is the pursuit of lost youth.

MRS. LIRRIPER

From *Mrs. Lirriper's Lodgings*

The novels of Charles Dickens have been read and loved for generations. This short story, like most of his writings, portray the people of London in the early nineteenth century. The following episode covers a portion of the yarn.

A chatty old soul is Mrs. Lirriper, as she confides to us the trials of running a lodging house.

Number eighty-one Norfolk Street, Strand—situated midway between the city and St. James's, and within five minutes walk of the principal places of public amusement—is my address. I have rented this house many years, so my landlord could testify were he alive. I remember that one. An old skinflint he was. Not a pound of paint nor as much as one tile upon the roof did he pay for.

My dear, you never find number eighty-one Norfolk Street, Strand advertised in Bradshaw's *Railway Guide*. And with the blessing of heaven, you never will. There are some who do not think it lowering themselves to make their names that cheap—and even going the lengths of putting a portrait of the house in it—with a coach and four at the door. But what will suit some like Miss Wozenham—she lives on the other side of the way—will not suit me. She has her opinions and I have mine. Though when it comes to underbidding, it can be proved by an oath in a court, that she says, "If Mrs. Lirriper names eighteen shillings a week, I name fifteen and six."

It is forty years ago since me and my poor Lirriper got married at St. Clement's Danes. I now have a pleasant pew there with genteel company, and my own hassock. I am partial to the evening service.

My poor Lirriper was a handsome figure of a man. He had a beaming eye, and a voice as mellow as a musical instrument. He was in the commerical traveling line. One night he set off on a trip with the dreadful horse that never would stand still for a single instant—even when the gate was shut. Off with the wheel, and my poor Lirriper and the gig were smashed to atoms.

After the funeral I went around to the creditors and I says, "Gentlemen, I am acquainted with the fact that I am not answerable for my late husband's debts, but I wish to pay them, for I am his lawful wife, and his good name is dear to me. I am going into the lodgings, gentlemen, as a business. If I prosper, every farthing that my late husband owed shall be paid for the sake of the love I bore him."

That took a long time until it was done. Then the

gentlemen presented me with a silver cream jug. It is engraved "To Mrs. Lirriper. A mark of grateful respect for her honorable conduct." It gave me quite a turn, it did, and almost too much for my feelings.

I am now an old woman and my good looks are gone. That's me, my dear, over the plate warmer. You took your chance having a portrait taken for fear people would be guessing it was somebody else. I remember there was a certain person that came in one morning to pay his rent. Well, he took it from the hook and said, "Speak to me, Emma!" That's my name. And he would have put it in his breast pocket had I not restrained him. So I like to think it was a likeness of me when I was young and wore that sort of stays.

But it was about the lodgings that I intended to hold forth. I certainly ought to know something of the business if all those years give wisdom.

Girls are your first trial. And the ones that try you even worse are what I call the Wandering Christians. They come in and view the apartments, stickle about the terms and never dream of taking them. It's wonderful they live so long and thrive so on it. But I suppose the exercise makes it healthy—knocking on so many doors, and going up and down stairs all day long. And then they pretend to be so particular and punctual. They look at their watches and say, "Could you give me the refusal of the room till twenty minutes past eleven the day after tomorrow?"

When I was new to it, my dear, I used to consider before I promised. But now I says, "Certainly, by all means." I know well enough it's a Wandering Christian and I shall hear no more about it. By this time I know most of the Wandering Christians by sight as well as they know me. It's a habit of them to come back about twice a year.

As I was about to remark, girls are one of your first and your lasting troubles when you are in this business. They are like your teeth which begin with convulsions and never cease to torment you from the time you cut them till they cut you. You don't want to part with them which seems hard—or buy artificial ones.

I would truly be thankful if I could trust all mankind. But alas, it is not so. When you are seeking lodgers and put a bill in the window about it, then don't keep your watch on the mantlepiece, and keep an eye on the sugar tongs. I have my reasons for saying so. Once a fine woman, I thought she was, got me to run for a glass of water, and when I came back she and the sugar tongs were missing.

My dear, I do assure you it's a harassing thing to know what kind of girls to give the preference to. If they are sluggish you suffer from it yourself by the complaints you hear. If they are sparkling-eyed they get made love to. If they are smart they try on your lodgers' bonnets.

And what the gentlemen like in girls the ladies

don't. But I can vow for it, one thing they do agree—they all want plenty of hot water.

When you go into the lodging business, my dear, you become the object of uncharitable suspicions. Never was I so dishonorable as to have two keys—like that Miss Wozenham. Lodgers open their minds to the idea that you are trying to get the better of them—and shut their minds to the idea that they are trying to get the better of you.

It is strange, my dear, the ways of people on this circular world.

PEASANT

From *What the Old Man Does Is Always Right*

The life of Hans Christian Andersen was strange and sad, similar to some of his stories. He was ugly in appearance, clumsy in manners, had little education, and failed in the theatre and as an operatic singer.

Even though his name became famous all over the world for his collection of tales, he still believed himself a failure because he had not made good in Copenhagen, the city of his choice.

This yarn has a bucolic charm and strange logic which reaps a golden reward. But suppose we allow the peasant, who was responsible for what happened, tell the story.

I suppose you have been in the country. Perhaps you have seen my farmhouse. It is very old and has a thatched roof. A stork's nest is on the summit of the gable—for we can't do without the stork. The walls of my house are sloping and the windows are so low that only one of them will open. We have an elder tree and a pool of water in which a few ducks disport themselves. In the yard is a dog who barks at all strangers.

There we live, my wife and I. Even though our property is small, we had an article that we could do without—a horse, which ate the grass by the side of the road. We thought it best if we sold the horse or exchanged it for something that might be more useful.

"But what might that something be?" I asked my wife.

She was sure I knew best about that. Since there was a fair in town that day, why didn't I ride there, get rid of the horse for money or make a good exchange. Whatever I did would be right with her.

So she fastened my neckerchief, brushed my hat with the palm of her hand, and gave me a kiss.

The sun shone hotly as I rode along the dusty road, for many people were driving, riding or walking to the fair.

I saw a man trudging along with a cow. It was as beautiful a creature as any cow can be. "She gives good milk, I'm sure," I said to myself. "That would be a good exchange—the cow for a horse."

"Hallo, you there with the cow!" I called to the man." I fancy a horse costs more than a cow. But a cow would be more useful to me. If you like, we'll exchange."

The man agreed and we exchanged accordingly. Now I might have turned back, for I had done the business I came to do, but I had made up my mind to go to the fair. So I went on to the town with the cow.

A short time later I overtook a man who was driving a sheep. It was a good fat sheep with fine fleece on its back. "I should like to have that fellow," I said. "He would find plenty of grass, and in the winter we could bring him in the room with us."

The man with the sheep was quite willing and the bargain was struck. So I walked along the road with a sheep.

Soon I saw a man coming from a field carrying a great goose under his arm.

"That's a heavy thing," I said to the man. "It has plenty of feathers and plenty of fat. It would look well tied to a string and paddling in the water at our place. Shall we exchange? I'll give you my sheep for your goose, and thank you into the bargain."

The man had no objection, so we exchanged, and I became proprietor of the goose.

By this time I was very near the town and the crowd on the road became greater and greater, so that for a time I walked in a potato field. I saw a fowl strutting about with a string tied to its legs so that it should not stray away and be lost. He had short-tailed feathers and winked with both his eyes.

"That's the finest fowl I've ever seen in my life!" I said. "Why it's finer than our parson's brood hen. On my word, I should like to have that fowl. It can always find a grain or two, and can almost keep itself."

When I asked the owner of the fowl if we should exchange, he agreed readily, and I went on my way with the fowl.

Now that I had done a good deal of business on my way to the fair, I was hot and tired. I wanted something to eat, and a glass of brandy to drink. Soon I was in front of an inn. I was just about to step inside when the hostler came out. He was carrying a sack.

"What have you in that sack?" I asked.

He replied it was a whole sackful of rotten apples —enough to feed the pigs with.

"Why, that's terrible waste! I should like to take them to my old woman at home. Last year the old tree only bore a single apple, and we kept it in the cupboard till it was quite rotten and spoiled."

Then the hostler asked what I would give for the sackful of rotten apples.

"I will give you my fowl in exchange."

So the bargain was made. I carried the bag inside, leaned it by the stove, and went to the table. Many guests were there, including two Englishmen who were so rich that their pockets bulged out with gold coins. The apples in the sack began to roast, for the stove was hot, and the gentlemen wished to know what was inside.

I told them the whole story of the horse that I had exchanged for a cow, and all the rest of it down to the apples.

They enjoyed the story but were sure that my old woman would give it to me when I got home.

"What? Give me what? She will kiss me and say, 'What the old man does is always right.'"

They could not believe that would happen, so they made a wager of a hundred pounds of gold that my old woman would make a disturbance.

"I can only set the bushel of apples against it. And I'll throw myself and my old woman into the bargain."

So the bet was made. And in a little while their carriage came along and we got in. Soon we stopped before my hut. The two Englishmen observed me as I greeted my wife.

"Good evening, old woman. I've made exchange," I began. "I got a cow in exchange for the horse."

She was pleased. Now we would have glorious milk, and butter and cheese upon the table.

"Yes, but I changed the cow for a sheep."

She thought that better still. We could have ewe's milk and cheese, woolen jackets and stockings.

"But I changed away the sheep for a goose."

Again she seemed pleased. Then we would have roast goose to eat.

"But I gave away the goose for a fowl."

That seemed a good exchange to her. The fowl would lay eggs and hatch them, and we would soon have chickens and a whole poultry yard.

"Yes, but I exchanged the fowl for a sack of shriveled apples."

She looked surprised. Well, for that she must positively kiss me. While I was away she had called to see the schoolmistress to borrow a handful of herbs. But the sad lady told her that nothing at all grew in her garden—not even a shriveled apple. Now we could lend the schoolmistress a whole sackful. My wife was indeed glad and gave me a sounding kiss.

The two Englishmen were astounded to see me kissed and not scolded. They agreed that was worth the hundred pounds of gold they paid me.

So you see it always pays when the wife sees and always asserts that her husband knows best—and that whatever he does is always right.

MR. THOMAS

From *The Tell-Tale Heart*

Edgar Allan Poe, as we know, specialized in writing stories of the macabre. This selection provides the necessary chills, and appropriately enough it all happens in a cheerless, shuttered house.

No proper names are given to any of the characters, so we will call our spokesman, Mr. Thomas, and assume he was a companion and secretary in the employ of an eccentric old man, Mr. Prindle, who was the owner of this forbidding house.

Mr. Thomas will tell us what happened in that eerie setting at four o'clock one winter morning.

I had retired shortly past midnight when I heard the shrill sound of a police whistle, and a moment later someone was rapping loudly upon the outer door. I slipped on my robe and slippers, turned up the lantern, and carried it with me toward the door. I said:

"Who is it? Who is there? Oh. A police officer. Just a minute until I unbolt the door."

I Step from a Famous Story

I cautiously opened the door. There stood two policemen.

"Come in, gentlemen. Yes, it is a very cold night.

"That's right. This is Mr. Prindle's house. My name is Thomas. I'm in Mr. Prindle's employ—as his secretary. He had a book shop—but because of poor health—a bad heart—he sold the business. But he kept me on—as a sort of companion, you might say.

"May I ask what brings you here? This is a most respectable neighborhood. Oh? Someone heard a scream and notified you. No, I don't recall hearing anything unusual.

"I see. Of course you may search the house. Follow me, gentlemen. As you see, we don't have many lamps about. Mr. Prindle prefers to live frugally. So I'll light the way as we go.

"No, I'm alone in the house. Mr. Prindle went to the country. A little visit with relatives. He left last evening and will be back in a few days, I expect.

"Here we are. This is Mr. Prindle's chamber. Let's sit here. I'll put this lantern on the table and we can gather around it. Comfortable? That's fine. I'll draw up this chair for myself.

"Now then—any more questions? No, I didn't venture out this evening. It was so cold and blustery that I stayed indoors. I read for a while, until it became too cold, and then I retired.

"Gentlemen, it just occurred to me. I believe I can

Mr. Thomas

offer the solution—about that scream. Excuse me for laughing, but I just recall. You see, I had a dream. I don't remember the details—but it was frightening—so that I screamed and woke up. I remember that part—that I screamed. So you see, officers, a dream accounts for it all. But I didn't realize that I screamed so loudly to disturb the neighbors. I'm sorry. It caused you a lot of trouble, I'm afraid.

"It is fortunate that Mr. Prindle isn't here. This visit of yours would have upset him. His heart, you know.

"So now you can return to headquarters—or wherever you go from here. I'm sorry I have no cigars to offer you. We're not accustomed to having guests. In fact, many people think this house is deserted. We always keep the shutters tightly closed.

"So if you officers wish to leave, I— Oh. No, I don't mind. Go ahead and search the house—if you still have doubts.

"Uh—what—what did you say? Can you speak a little louder?

"What time is it? A few minutes past four. It—it's getting chilly in here. Let's leave this room and— Please. Why do you keep sitting there when—

"There. It's getting louder. There's a ringing in my ears. I—I think I'd better go to bed. I'm feverish. So excuse me if I—

"Listen! Don't you hear it? That awful ticking—

like a watch wrapped in cotton. There it is again. Don't you hear it? You lie! You must hear it. It's getting louder—louder!

"Oh, why do you keep on talking like that? It doesn't make sense. I can't hear you because of that terrible ticking. And yet your lips are moving. Stop talking, will you? And go—for God's sake. Go—go quickly. Oh, why do you sit there smiling like that? You fancy me mad, don't you? I'm not! I'm not! If only that ticking would stop! It's beating louder now—like a hammer striking an anvil.

"I know what it is—that terrible ticking. Do you hear? I know what it is. But you don't. You're a fine pair. There you sit—two stupid officers of the law—and you find nothing.

"You fools! Must I tell you what it is? Yes, I will—I must. Perhaps then it will stop.

"Listen to me. Come closer. I can't talk louder. I—I did it. I killed the old man—Mr. Prindle—tonight. Yes, I murdered him. Oh, don't ask stupid questions. Just listen. I must talk fast so that it'll stop.

"To do this thing has haunted me for a long time. It was well planned—and tonight I had to do it. I didn't want his filthy gold. It was his eye. That's what made me do it. Oh! I'll always see that eye. It was like that of a vulture—pale blue with a hideous film over it. Oh! It chilled the very marrow in my bones to look on it. I took his life so that I could rid myself of that evil eye forever.

"And so—at midnight—I opened the door of his chamber. That door there. The room was black. I opened the lantern which I carried just a little, but in doing it my hand slipped against the tin. The old man heard the noise. He sat up in bed and cried out, 'Who's there?' I said nothing. For a whole hour I stood there, never moving a muscle. Then I opened the lantern a little further—and a ray of light fell upon that awful eye. It was wide open. Oh! I'll never forget it. And then I heard a dull sound—beating—beating—beating. I knew what it was. It was the beating of the old man's heart. It grew louder—louder. I couldn't stand it any longer. With a yell I threw open the lantern and leaped into the room. He cried out—only once. I—I dragged him to the floor, pulled the heavy bed on top of him—and that ended it all. In a little while he was dead—stone dead.

"But you couldn't find the body, could you? I was too clever for you. Listen. Can't you hear it? Hark! There it is again. Louder—louder—louder!

"There—there—where I'm pointing. Tear up the planks in the floor. Hurry, hurry! Hear it? Now do you know what it is? It's the beating of his hideous heart."

THE MARQUISE DE R——

From *The Marquise*

The name of George Sand is recognized as the nom de plume of a talented authoress who was born in Paris in 1804. Her pseudonym is easy to remember in comparison to her full name—Amandine Lucile Aurore Dupin Dudevant.

This story of the eighteenth century illustrates the illusion of the stage with its actors who play parts, and who sometimes do it so convincingly, that their art can stir the hearts of even royalty.

Sitting on an elegant chair within the opulence of her apartment, an elderly Marquise confides to an old friend.

As you know, I am a genuine Marquise, and have seen the Court of Louis XV. I had the misfortune to be beautiful, as that portrait over there reveals. As you see, it represents me in the character of a huntress, with a low satin waist painted to imitate tiger-skin, and a crescent of pearls to light up my hair.

I am now eighty years of age. My dear friend, the Viscomte de Larrieux, has just died of the gout. Several of my friends have gone this year. And although I tell myself that I am younger and stronger than any of them, I cannot help being frightened when I see my contemporaries dropping off around me.

It is the opinion of some that I am cold and heartless. I shall let you judge. Then, I shall at least not die without having made myself known to someone.

When I was sixteen I left St. Cyr, where I had been educated, to marry the Marquis de R——. He was fifty, but I dared not complain, for every one congratulated me on so splendid a match.

I was never very bright, and at that time I was positively stupid. The education of the cloister had completely benumbed my faculties. I left the convent with a romantic idea of life and of the world.

I was a widow before I was seventeen, and as soon as I was out of mourning I was surrounded by suitors. I was then in all the splendor of my beauty, and it was generally admitted that there was neither face nor figure that could compare with mine. But my husband, an old, dissipated man, who had never shown me anything but irony and disdain, and had married me only to secure an office promised with my hand, had left me an aversion to marriage. In my ignorance of life, I fancied that all men resembled him. I boldly declared that I despised all men. There is nothing men will resent more readily than this.

Then I was presented to the Viscomte de Larrieux, who loved me sincerely. He ate with delight, fell asleep in all the armchairs, and the remainder of the time he took snuff. He was always occupied in satisfying some appetite. I never had the energy to get rid of him, so for sixty years he was my torment.

But since I have begun my confessions, I will acknowledge that once, and only once, I have loved with a passion that was ideal.

For you see, if many old women of eighty were to tell the history of their lives, you would find that the feminine soul contains sources of good and evil.

And now, guess what was the rank of the man for whom I entirely lost my head? The King of France, you say?

No indeed. Perhaps I better tell you at once. He was an actor. The noblest, the most elegant that ever trod the boards.

The first time I saw him I expressed my admiration to the Comtesse de Ferriers. She cautioned me to speak not so warmly, that I should not forget that in the eyes of a woman of rank, an actor can never be a man.

His name was Lelio. He was by birth an Italian, but spoke French admirably. He may have been thirty-five, but on the stage he often seemed less than twenty. He played Corneille and Racine and was admirable in both.

He was never famous, and was appreciated neither by the court nor the town. I have heard that he was outrageously hissed when he first appeared. Afterward he was valued for his feeling, his fire, and his efforts at correct elocution. He was tolerated and sometimes applauded, but on the whole, he was always considered an actor without taste.

In those days tragedy was played "properly." It was necessary to die with taste, to fall gracefully, and to have an air of good breeding even in the case of a blow. Dramatic art was modeled upon the usage of good society, and the diction and gestures of the actors were in harmony with the hoops and hair powder. I have never appreciated the defects of this school of art. I bravely endured it twice in the week, for it was the fashion to like it.

One evening, after a rather long absence from Paris, I went to the Comédie Française to see *Le Cid*. Lelio had been admitted to this theatre during my stay in the country, and I saw him for the first time. He played Rodrigue.

I was deeply moved by the very first tone of his voice. It was penetrating rather than sonorous, but vibrating and strongly accentuated. His voice was much criticized. That of the Cid was supposed to be deep and powerful, just as all the heroes of antiquity were supposed to be tall and strong. A king who was but five feet six inches could not wear the diadem; it would have been contrary to the decrees of tastes.

Lelio was small and slender. His beauty lay not in the features, but in the nobleness of his forehead, the irresistible grace of his attitude, the careless ease of his movements, the proud but melancholy expression of his face. The word *charm* should have been invented for him.

It was indeed a charm which he threw around me. This man, who stepped, spoke, moved without system of affectation, who sobbed with his heart as much as with his voice, who forgot himself to become identified with his passion, cast over me a magnetic power. For five years he was my king, my life, my love. To me he was much more than a man. His was an intellectual power which formed my soul at his will.

Soon I was unable to conceal the impression he made on me. I gave up my box at the Comédie Française in order not to betray myself. I pretended I had become pious, and that in the evening I went to pray in the churches. Instead of that, I dressed myself as a working woman and mingled with the common people so that I might listen to him unconstrained. I gave full play to my emotions. I shouted, I wept, I passionately called his name. Happily for me, my weak voice was drowned in the storm which raged about me.

At other times he was hissed when he seemed to me to be sublime, and then I would leave the theatre, my heart full of rage.

One evening as I left the theatre by the side passage, a small, slender man passed in front of me and turned into the street. One of the stage carpenters took off his hat and said: "Good evening, Monsieur Lelio."

Eager to obtain a closer view of this extraordinary man, I ran after him, and followed him into a café. Fortunately, it was not one in which I was likely to meet any one of my own rank.

When, by the light of the smoky lamp, I looked at Lelio, I thought I had been mistaken and had followed another man. He was at least thirty-five, sallow, withered. He was badly dressed, he looked vulgar, spoke in a hoarse voice, shook hands with the meanest wretches, drank brandy, and swore horribly.

It was not until I had heard his name repeated several times that I felt sure that this was the divinity of the theatre, the interpreter of the great Corneille. I could recognize none of those charms which had so fascinated me. His eyes were dull; his strongly accentuated pronunciation seemed ignoble when he called to the waiter or talked of gambling and taverns. He walked badly, he looked vulgar, and the paint was only half wiped from his cheeks. It was no longer Hippolyte—it was Lelio. The temple was empty; the oracle was dumb; the divinity had become a man, not even a man—an actor.

I sat stupefied without even presence of mind to drink the hot spiced wine I had called for.

When I awoke the next morning in my own bed

with its wadded curtains and coronet of pink feathers, I almost thought I had dreamed, and felt greatly mortified when I recollected the disillusions of the previous night.

I thought myself thoroughly cured of my love, and I tried to rejoice at it, but in vain. I was filled with mortal regret, and again the weariness of life entered my heart.

About a week later, the Comtesse de Ferriers came to see me and remarked that I was no longer seen at the theatre. She said Lelio had improved and was sometimes applauded. I allowed myself to be persuaded to accompany her to the performance that evening, even though I was completely disenchanted with Lelio. I dressed myself with excessive brilliance.

Sitting in our court proscenium box, I was aware that Lelio noticed me, either on account of my dress or my emotions. Several times during the play his eyes turned toward me.

That night I understood for the first time the nature of the passion which enchanted me to Lelio. It was not he I loved, but those heroes of ancient times whose sincerity, whose fidelity, whose tenderness he knew how to portray; with him and by him I was carried back to an epoch of forgotten virtues. The illusions of the stage, the glare of the footlights, were a part of the being whom I loved. Without them he was nothing to me, and faded like a story before the brightness of day. I had no desire to see him off the boards. It would have been like contemplating the ashes of a great man.

Then I changed my box to a smaller one, less in view of the house, and better situated. I was almost upon the stage. I did not lose one of Lelio's glances, and he could look at me without it being seen by the public. His signs, the expression which he gave to certain words, told me that he was speaking to me. I was the happiest and proudest of women, for then it was the hero, not the actor, who loved me.

One day I read in the *Mercure de France* the name of a new actor engaged at the Comédie Française to replace Lelio, who was about to leave France. This announcement was a mortal blow to me. I could not conceive how I should exist when deprived of these emotions, this life of passion.

While I was in this state, I received a letter in an unknown hand. I shall show it to you. It is over here in this inlaid box. You see how crumpled it is from much reading.

In it, he asks pardon for his boldness in writing, but he had to reveal his love for me. He was aware of my rank of pomp and splendor while he was an obscure and nameless artist. But he had the consoling thought that had he been born in the same rank, I would have been his.

I was overwhelmed by the letter. In my reply I accused destiny, that pride could not make me deny that I felt a preference for him. That was the only consolation I could offer him.

Next day I received a note. In it he pleaded to see me or he would die. We exchanged a few notes, and a meeting place was arranged—a house in the Rue de Valois at midnight.

I dressed simply, put no ornaments in my hair, and refused to wear rouge. Carefully veiled, I was in the concert room in that house, waiting for Lelio. The soft, even light might have been mistaken for that of the moon.

Suddenly a door was opened and closed, and light footsteps sounded upon the floor. I sank into a chair, for I was about to see Lelio shorn of the illusions of the stage. I closed my eyes for a moment, then reopened them.

But how much was I surprised! Lelio was beautiful as an angel. He had not taken off his stage dress, and it was the most elegant I had ever seen him wear. His Spanish doublet was of white satin, his shoulder and garter knots of cherry ribbons, and a short cloak of the same color was thrown over his shoulder. He wore an immense ruff of English lace, his hair was short and unpowdered, partially covered by a cap with white feathers and a diamond rose. In this costume he had just played Don Juan. Never had I seen him so beautiful, so young, so poetical as at that moment.

He knelt before me and covered my hand with

kisses. My senses seemed to desert me, as I caressed his burning forehead, his black hair, and wept delicious tears.

Then he told me how from a dissipated actor I had made him a man full of life and ardor; how I had raised him in his own eyes and restored to him the illusions of his youth. Never did Racine make love utter itself with such poetry, such strength.

I threw my arms around his neck, touched the satin of his coat, as I breathed the perfume of his hair.

"Listen, Lelio," I said. "I swear to love you till my death. The snows of age will not have the power to extinguish this ardent love. Let us carry from this place a whole future of blissful thoughts and adored memories. Find happiness in thinking of me."

The carriage I had sent for arrived. In despair, Lelio threw himself in front of the door and passionately entreated me never to leave him, but I gently repulsed him. He yielded as I crossed the threshold and walked away a few steps. I was about to lose him forever. I turned back and looked at him once more. Despair had crushed him. He was old, altered, frightful. His body seemed paralyzed. His stiffened lips attempted an unmeaning smile. His eyes were glassy and dim. He was now only Lelio, the shadow of a lover and a prince.

There you have my whole history. Do you not now believe in the ideality of the eighteenth century?

MR. MARKHEIM

From *Markheim*

The life of Robert Louis Stevenson was almost a constant journey in search of adventure, even though he was suffering from tuberculosis which afflicted him during childhood.

The desperate young man of this story cannot be admired for a hero, as he commits an act of violence in the following scene. It happened in an art dealer's shop in London.

I had an urgent reason for paying a call to that shop—even though it was Christmas day and I knew the shutters would be closed. But if I persisted in ringing the bell, the dealer might open, if only to inquire my business. I would have a ready answer for that—even though it was a deliberate lie. He would remember me. From time to time I had brought in various curios that my uncle wished to sell.

I rang the bell many times before the key turned and the partially opened door revealed the pale, round-shouldered dealer. He greeted me gruffly and was reluctant to admit me.

"Yes, I know this is a strange time to call—on Christmas day—when your shutters are closed. But grumble no longer, for this time I have not come to sell but to buy."

"I have done well on the Stock Exchange lately, so my errand today is simplicity itself. I seek a Christmas present for a lady. I am sorry to disturb you upon so small a matter. But I neglected to buy it yesterday and I must produce my little compliment at dinner. As you very well know, a rich marriage is not a thing to be neglected."

A ticking of many clocks filled in the pause as the dealer weighed my statement. Then, grudgingly, he led the way into the room. He picked up a hand mirror, one from the fifteenth century, as a suitable present. His dry and biting voice irritated me. I looked at the mirror with disdain.

"A glass? For Christmas? Surely not!" I grabbed the mirror from him and held it before the ugly face. "You ask me why not? Here, look in it. Look at yourself! Do you like to see it? No! Nor I, nor any man. I ask you for a Christmas present and you give me this —this damned reminder of years, and sins, and follies. It is a hand-conscience!"

He sharply replied that I should make my purchase or walk out of his shop. I realized that I had been too blunt. I would assume a friendly manner.

"Why the haste?" I asked, with a cordial tone. "It is very pleasant to stand here talking—and life is so short and insecure that I would not hurry away from any pleasure—not even so mild a one as this. Let us be confidential. Who knows, we might become friends. But since you wish me to make a purchase at once, show me something else."

The dealer stooped to replace the mirror upon the shelf.

I felt a sudden repulsion for the grouchy old man. For my purposes I would have to dispose of him. I reached in my coat pocket and withdrew a dagger. One thrust of it was enough. With a feeble gasp, the man reeled back, struck his head on the shelf, and then tumbled to the floor.

On the counter a candle burned. Shadows nodded on the faces of the portraits hanging on the walls. Fear-stricken, my eyes returned to the body of the victim in its miserly clothes. The clocks began to strike. It was the hour of three in the afternoon. I picked up the candle, then moved about the room as I filled my pockets with pieces of jewelry.

My mind began to accuse me of the faults of my deed. I should not have used a dagger. I should have been more cautious and only bound and gagged the man—not killed him. I had other alarms. Perhaps a neighbor saw me enter the shop and was watching by the window for my departure. But through the brick walls and shuttered windows only sounds could penetrate—and the death cry was feeble indeed.

Mr. Markheim

I knew I was alone in the house. From across the street I had watched when the servant in her poor best, had hurried away. And yet, I could hear a stir of footsteps. Another presence seemed to be about. It was a faceless thing, and yet had eyes to see with. Surely it must be my imagination.

Suddenly, from the street outside, I heard the beat of a stick on the door and a man's voice shouted out the name of the dealer. I was smitten into ice. I glanced at the dead man. He lay quite still. He was beyond earshot of those blows and shoutings. Then, after repeated calls and rappings, the sound was heard no more.

I had to hurry—attend to what had to be done— then get away from this accusing neighborhood. In a half hour I hoped to plunge into the London multitudes and reach that haven of safety—my bed. One visitor had come. At any moment another might follow. To get the money was my immediate concern. For that I needed the keys—and those would be on the person of the slain man.

I shivered as my hands touched the body and turned it on its back. It was strangely light and supple. The face was robbed of all expression—but was as pale as wax, and smeared with blood about the forehead. I found the keys in one of his pockets. Then I advanced toward the door which led to the other rooms of the house.

Outside, it had begun to rain and the sound of the

shower upon the roof banished the silence. As I approached the door, I seemed to hear in answer to my own cautious tread, the steps of other feet withdrawing up the stairs.

The sense that I was not alone grew upon me. On every side I was haunted by presences. I heard them moving in the upper chambers. From the shop, I heard the dead man getting to his legs. As I began with a great effort to mount the stairs, feet fled before me and followed stealthily behind me. The four-and-twenty steps to the first floor seemed like four-and-twenty agonies.

I got safely into the drawing room and shut the door behind me. The room was strewn with packing cases, furniture of all periods, many pictures framed and unframed. By good fortune the shutters at the windows had been closed, so I was concealed from any prying neighbors. I tried to open a cabinet but discovered it was locked. I tried the various keys.

All at once I was startled by the sound of steps mounting the stairs. A flash of ice, then a flash of fire went over me as I stood there transfixed. Then I saw the knob turn and the door opened.

What was I to expect? Was the dead man walking —or was it a witness who had seen the terrible deed and would turn me over to the gallows? Then a face was thrust into the opening. It glanced around the room, looked at me, nodded and smiled as if in recognition. Then it withdrew and the door closed behind it.

"Who—who are you?" I cried out hoarsely.

The vision returned. Then a voice asked if I had called him.

I gazed in wonder—but the outlines of the newcomer seemed to change and waver. At times I thought I knew him—at times he had a likeness to me. I felt a living terror that this was not of the earth and not of God.

With a smile he informed me that if I was looking for the money I would have to hurry, as the maid had left her sweetheart earlier than usual and would be back shortly. I was astonished when he addressed me by name.

"You know me?" I cried. "What are you? The devil?"

He evaded the question, saying that he had a service to render me.

"Be helped by you? No, never—not by you. You do not know me yet. Thank God you do not know me!"

But he replied that he knew me to the soul.

"Know me! Who knows himself? My life is but a travesty and slander on myself. I have lived to belie my nature. You would judge me by my acts! But can you not look within? Can you not understand that evil is hateful to me? Can you not read me for what must be common in humanity—the unwilling sinner?"

But the image stated that I should continue to please myself in life—that I could make a confession on my deathbed.

I resented such a remark. "Do you suppose me such a creature? To sin, and sin, and sin and at the last sneak into heaven? I will lay my heart open to you. This crime on which you find me is my last."

Then he reminded me that I wanted to use the money on the Stock Exchange, when I had already lost some thousands.

"That's true. But this time I have a sure thing." But he assured me that I would again lose it. "Ah, but I will keep back the half." That I would also lose, he predicted.

Sweat started upon my brow. "Well then, say I am plunged again in poverty. Evil and good run strong in me. Are my vices only to direct my life? My virtues, are they to lie without effect?"

Then he raised a finger and pointed downward. That was my way—downward. Only death would stop me.

Before I could reply, the sharp note of the doorbell rang through the house.

It was the maid, the vision said. I could go downstairs, open the door, admit her, and when she saw the body, I could say that her master was ill. Then I could use the same skill upon her that I performed

Mr. Markheim

on the dealer to get rid of him. Then I would have the whole evening free to ransack the treasures of the house.

I hesitated before answering. "If my life be an ill thing, I can lay it down. I have still my hatred of evil. That will give me the courage to atone for my wickedness."

The features of the vision seemed to brighten, as if pleased by my resolution. Then it disappeared.

But I had no time to delay. As I went downstairs, my thoughts brought my past soberly before me. I beheld it as ugly—a scene of defeat.

I looked into the shop where the candle still burned by the dead body. The bell rang out again with an impatient clamor.

I opened the door and said to the maid: "You had better go for the police. I have killed your master."

MISS MARY

From *The Idyl of Red Gulch*

The name of Bret Harte recalls the colorful tales of the west in the "gold rush" era. Although he grew up in Albany and New York, at the age of eighteen he moved to California, which accounts for the authentic flavor of his stories.

Among the shadows of pine trees, and the puffs of red dust raised by the plunging hoofs of passing teams, is the setting of the opening scene.

A young lady, called Miss Mary by her little flock of pupils, had closed the door of the log schoolhouse and was taking her afternoon walk.

I usually chose the same path each day. It was particularly attractive with all the spring flowers bursting with their radiance. On that afternoon I crossed the road to reach for a cluster of azalea blossoms—when a strange sight caused me to scream. A man was lying on the ground. A quick glance told me he was in a drunken stupor. A hat was by his side. With a sudden spurt of courage, I picked it up and placed the hat over his face. That would

Miss Mary

shield him from the sun. But as I did so, I noticed that his eyes were open. I quickly moved away a few steps, then looked back, and noticed that the hat was again by his side. With fresh boldness I asked:

"Is—is anything the matter?"

When he mumbled something I became incensed. "Get up, you horrid man. Get up and go home."

No sooner had I said that, when he staggered to his feet. He was at least six feet tall. I trembled as he started toward me. Eyeing his grimy appearance, I said: "Go and take a bath."

With that he suddenly pulled off his coat and vest, threw them on the ground, then kicked off his boots and darted over the hill in the direction of the river. I watched with dismay. "Good heavens! The man will be drowned!" Then for some strange reason, I ran back to the schoolhouse and locked myself in.

That night while having supper with Mrs. Stidger —I had a room and board in her house—I suddenly asked: "Mrs. Stidger, does—does your husband ever get drunk?" He was a blacksmith.

She reflected for a moment then said that he hadn't been tight since last election. I would have liked to ask if lying in the sun and then taking a cold bath was helpful in that condition. But I didn't venture such questions.

For the next few days I took my afternoon walks in another direction. I noticed that every morning a fresh cluster of azalea blossoms was on my desk. This was not strange as my little flock knew my fondness for flowers, and they always kept my desk bright with them. But when I wanted to thank the pupil who brought the azaleas, no one spoke up.

Several days later, Master Johnny Stidger, whose desk was nearest the window, was suddenly taken with a spasm of laughter. All that he would say was that someone had been looking in the "winder."

Indignant that a prowler was about, I marched to the door. Outside, looking perfectly sober and sheepish, was the drunken man I had encountered about a week ago. I must admit he was amiable looking. He reminded me of a blond Samson. His corn-colored, silken beard had not been touched by a barber's razor or Delilah's shears. The cutting speech that I was prepared to give died upon my lips as he stammered an apology. I merely nodded and returned to the school room. So he was the mysterious courier who brought the azaleas. I didn't even know his name. Johnny informed me that everyone called him Sandy.

Soon after that—on a hot afternoon—I sent two of the boys to the spring to return with a pail of water. As they scampered back, most of it was spilled along the way. I realized that I had better get it myself. Just as I reached the foot of the hill on the way back, a shadow crossed my path. Without saying a word, Sandy reached for the bucket and walked along with me.

Miss Mary

I was both embarrassed and angry. "If you carried more of that for yourself, you'd do better." But when I took a sly glance at him and noticed his penitent expression, I regretted my sharp speech. But I did thank him as sweetly as I could when we reached the door, which caused him to stumble. That made the children laugh, and I admit I joined in.

The next day another surprise awaited me. A barrel filled with spring water was placed beside the door. Every morning it was replenished with fresh water. Another contribution from Sandy.

I remember the day I had planned a picnic on Buckeye Hill for the children. It was so lovely to be away from the dusty road with its straggling shanties. Soon I was running, laughing and panting with the pupils. And who should we discover in the heart of the forest but Sandy.

He tried to explain and apologize, but I interrupted with a smile. In no time he was accepted as one of the party. Before long he was the center of attention as he built a fire against a tree. And when he showed them other mysteries of woodcraft, their admiration was boundless. Then he flung himself on the ground and watched as I wove a wreath of laurel and mock orange.

Overhead the woodpeckers chattered, and from the hollow below sounded the happy voices of the children. Sandy took me in his confidence as he spoke about himself. He was an orphan who came to

California for excitement. He had led a wild life but he was trying to reform. Then I told him that I was an orphan also, and had left my uncle's home in Boston to go west to improve my health. All too soon it was time to take the children back. But that afternoon will remain a fond memory.

And then, before I had time to realize it, the long dry summer set in, and the school term was over until fall. Little did I suspect that something would happen on my last day of school which would affect my future.

I was alone in the room, seated at my desk, lost in thoughts about my stay in Red Gulch and the trip I would take tomorrow. I would miss the pupils—but even more so I was aware how much I had enjoyed my afternoon walks with Sandy. He would be here, waiting for me in September—but could I depend on his word? He might seek another town for some new adventure.

My reverie was interrupted by the sound of tapping at the door. I was surprised to see an overdressed woman standing there. I recognized her as the mother of Tommy, one of my pupils. The town whispered wicked gossip about her manner of living. She called herself Mrs. Robbins, but no one seemed to recall a Mr. Robbins. In her lilac-colored glove she held a parasol. Her painted face had a friendly, almost timid expression.

"Oh, Mrs. Robbins. Won't you come in? School

Miss Mary 55

was dismissed over an hour ago. So Tommy isn't here." But she called to speak to me. I answered a few questions.

"Yes, I am leaving here tomorrow. I want to visit my uncle in Boston.

"Oh, that's very nice of you to thank me for being kind to Tommy. He is a good boy and deserved whatever I could give him."

I was impressed how devoted she felt toward Tommy. She was here to ask me a favor—not for herself—but for her darling boy. She wanted the proper person to bring him up—and mentioned that Tommy loved me and talked about me so much. I was startled when she implored me to take him away. She had plenty of money, she assured me, so that I could put him in a good school where I could go and see him, and help him to forget his mother. She begged me to take Tommy away from his home of shame and sorrow. When he was grown up, then I should tell him the name of his father. It was a name that had not passed her lips for years.

"And what name is that?" I asked. "Alexander Morton," I repeated. "You say they call him Sandy? Oh."

I felt numb. The name Sandy re-echoed in my ears. The woman grasped my hand, but I broke away and walked to the window. Why did I listen to this sinful woman when it would end my friendship with Sandy? Again she pleaded for me to consider and not deny her.

"Very well. I will take the boy. Send him to me tonight."

In gratitude she knelt beside me.

"This man—does he know your intentions?" She said he did not and had never seen the child to know about it.

"Then go to him tonight. Tell him what you have done. Tell him I have taken his child. Make him promise that he must never see the boy. Wherever it may be, he must not come—wherever I may take Tommy, he must not follow. And now will you go, please? I—I am rather weary—and I have a lot to do."

She pressed a purse in my hand. We walked together to the door. And then to reassure the woman, I reached out and embraced her for a moment.

The next morning Tommy and I sat on the back seat of the stage coach. As we passed a certain azalea bush, I asked the driver to stop. Then I said to Tommy: "Tommy, will you run over there and cut off a branch of that azalea bush?"

Eager to obey, he whipped out his new pocket knife and followed my instructions before he returned to the coach. I held the branch close to me as we clattered away.

DORIAN GRAY

From *The Picture of Dorian Gray*

This short novel by Oscar Wilde when it first appeared in 1891, was discussed in whispers and with raised eyebrows. Its theme of decadence was rather shocking for a timid reader. A compelling plot and dazzling style is still intriguing for modern diversion.

By glancing at the apparent radiance of Dorian Gray, it is difficult to imagine that his life was to have such a tragic and grotesque end. But let him relate what events led to his strange destiny.

It was bantered about by the fashionable set in London, that the gods were good to me. I had youth—my manner was one of easy grace—I could be charming—and my face inspired a portrait. Aside from all those gifts, I lived in luxury as a result of a generous inheritance. Yet at the age of twenty, I accepted life as a simple schoolboy, and my pleasures were simple and proper.

One day at a small party at Lady Brandon's, I met Basil Hallward, a noted painter. He wanted to capture my youth on canvas. So he invited me to his studio to sit for a portrait.

I recall the afternoon it was finished. Basil put down his brush and asked me to look at it. My cheeks flushed with pleasure as I recognized myself for the first time—aware of the beauty that I had always dismissed. Basil could see by my expression that I liked it, and proudly called it his masterpiece. After a few moments of studying it, I said:

"How sad it is. I shall grow old and horrible and dreadful. But that picture will remain always young. It will never be older than this particular day in June. If it were only the other way! If it were I who was to be always young and the picture that was to grow old. For that—for that—I would give everything! Yes, there is nothing in the whole world I would not give! I would give my soul for that!"

My outburst rather shocked Basil. But I continued:

"I know now that when one loses one's good looks, one loses everything. Your picture has taught me that. Youth is the only thing worth having. When I find that I am growing old, I shall kill myself."

Basil did his best to comfort me. Then he very generously presented the picture to me.

I soon recovered from my morbid mood. In the studio that afternoon I met Lord Henry Wotton, a friend of Basil's. His debonair, worldly manner fascinated me. He encouraged me to become more curious about life. I realized that had been an inner desire of mine for a long time but I had never expressed it.

I wanted to experience more than elegant social affairs. So I lounged in the Park or strolled down Piccadilly, looking at everyone who passed me and wondered with a mad curiosity what sort of life they led.

In search of adventure, I would take a hansom to the grimy sections of the city, and there in a tawdry theatre, I lost my heart to the girl with the flower-like face who played Juliet. Her name was Sibyl Vane. I went back every evening and saw her appear as Desdemona, Rosalind, Portia, Ophelia. We met after every performance and she became the great romance of my life. I was so enthused about her ability as an actress, that I persuaded Basil and Lord Henry to accompany me. But that evening she gave a dreadful, artificial performance—and I realized she had killed my love.

Afterward, when I met her in the greenroom, she seemed joyful of her bad acting. The reason for it was her sudden discovery of the reality of her love for me, she explained. She hated the stage—all of a sudden it seemed artificial. She no longer wanted to be a puppet of a play—and she begged me to take her away. I spurned her emotional display and emphatically said that I would never see her again. She wept as I rushed out of the theatre.

When I returned home and was on my way to the bedroom, I passed through the library. My eye fell upon the portrait Basil had painted of me. I stopped suddenly and stared at it in surprise. There was something different about it. The expression around the mouth—it had a touch of cruelty. How strange. Did this portrait have some magic power to reveal my soul?

It was long past noon when I awoke the next day. Victor, my valet, brought a cup of tea. I had a change of heart about Sibyl. I had been selfish and cruel to her. I would go back to her.

As soon as I was dressed I went into the library. What I saw last evening—was it true? Had the portrait really changed? Or had it been my imagination that made me see a look of evil where there had been a look of joy? It was absurd to think a painted canvas could alter. I locked the door—then turned toward the painting. Yes, it was perfectly true. The portrait had altered.

Suddenly there came a knock on the door and I heard Lord Henry's voice outside. He insisted that I see him. Hastily, I put a screen across the picture and unlocked the door. He didn't appear his usual jaunty self and murmured that he was sorry.

"You mean about Sibyl, I suppose?" I asked. "I was brutal to her. I will write a letter imploring her forgiveness. I want to marry Sibyl."

Lord Henry looked shocked. Then he told me the

horrible news. It was in the morning paper. Sibyl was found lying dead on the floor of her dressing room. She had swallowed something by mistake, it said—something that actresses use—which contained prussic acid.

I knew it was suicide. I had murdered Sibyl Vane as surely as if I had cut her throat with a knife. It had all the terrible beauty of a Greek tragedy. A tragedy in which I took a giant part but by which I was not wounded. I realized why I had loved her. She had represented to me all the heroines of romance. But she had no right to kill herself. It was selfish of her. Lord Henry consoled me, and before he left I had promised to join him at the opera that evening.

I rushed to the screen and drew it back. No, there was no further change in the picture. The line of vicious cruelty had no doubt appeared at the very moment Sibyl had drunk the poison. The portrait could not remain in the library. It had to be hidden away.

I sent for the housekeeper and requested the key to the attic room. Then throwing a purple, satin coverlet over the picture, I told Victor to carry it upstairs. I accompanied him, to see that he didn't pry. The key to that room would always be in my possession.

There. It was in a safe place. It would never tempt me again. If the picture was to alter so be it. And so I fulfilled my passion for sensations. I visited ill-famed taverns near the Docks. I cavorted with thieves, and satisfied my desire for opium. My mad hungers grew more ravenous as I fed them.

My name became the chatter of gentlemen at clubs. All sorts of curious stories circulated about me. Some of my friends would pass me by with a sneer.

Yet I had the look of one who kept himself unspotted from the world. Even on my thirty-eighth birthday I had kept the purity of face. Many young men envied me and copied my mode of dress. And I still had the choice to accept or decline many social functions.

Often, on returning home after a mysterious absence, I would creep upstairs to the locked room. There I would hold a mirror as I stood before the portrait. I'd look at the evil, ageing face on the canvas—then turn to look at the fair, young face that laughed back at me from the polished glass.

Then one evening after walking home from Lord Henry's residence at Grosvenor Square, a man carrying a Gladstone bag passed me in the mist. Then he hurried after me. It was Basil. I had not seen him for many months. He was going to Paris by the midnight train, but had something urgent to tell me. I invited him to return home with me.

"What is it all about?" I asked. "I hope it is not about myself. I am tired of myself tonight. I should like to be somebody else." I lit one of my gold-tipped cigarettes and listened.

"So they are saying dreadful things about me. I don't wish to know about them. I love scandals about other people—but scandals about myself bore me. They have no charm of novelty.

"Oh. So I am to blame when others do miserable deeds—just because they once were friends of mine? I taught them vices, did I? Ask those people who told you this—what sort of lives do they lead? My dear fellow, you forget we are in the native land of the hypocrite.

"I'm glad you said that, Basil—that sin writes itself across a man's face. Look at mine.

"You'd have to see my soul!" I laughed bitterly. "Very well. You shall see it yourself, tonight." I seized a lamp from the table. "Come, Basil. It is in your handiwork. You have chattered enough about corruption. Now you shall look at it face to face."

The lamp cast fantastic shadows on the wall as we ascended the staircase. A rising wind made the windows rattle. I unlocked the door, entered the cluttered room and Basil followed. I placed the lamp on the table.

"Shut the door behind you," I whispered. He did so. "So you think that it is only God who sees the soul? Draw that curtain back and you will see mine. You hestitate. Then I must do it myself. There.

"You look startled. Look again. It's your picture—

and I was your ideal. Can't you see it there?" I taunted.

"You ask what it means? Let me recall for you. Years ago, when I was a boy, you met me, flattered me, and taught me to be vain about my good looks. In a mad moment, that even now I don't know whether I regret or not, I made a wish. Remember? So there it is, Basil—the face of my soul."

Looking at the horrible picture I felt an uncontrolled hatred for Basil Hallward. I glanced wildly about. Something glimmered on the top of a chest. It was a knife. I rushed at him and dug the knife into the great vein behind the ear, pushed his head on the table and stabbed again and again. He uttered only one stifled groan. Then something began to trickle on the floor.

By the next morning I knew what I had to do about disposing of the body that was locked in the upstairs room. Alan Campbell was the man to do it. We had been great friends once—then for some reason he chose to avoid me. He was devoted to chemistry and had a laboratory of his own. I sent Victor to his address with a letter. The message was urgent—that it was a matter of life and death. Within an hour, Alan, looking very stern, was ushered into the library.

"Alan! This is kind of you! I thank you for coming. Sit down."

After a strained moment of silence, I said: "Alan, in a locked room in the attic, a dead man is seated at a table. He has been dead for ten hours now. At this moment he is supposed to be in Paris. He will not be missed for months. When he is missed there must be no trace of him found here. You know about chemistry and things of that kind. You, Alan, must change him and everything that belongs to him, into a handful of ashes that I may scatter in the air."

He protested strongly. He had no desire to help me. My devil's work had nothing to do with him. I tried to reason with him—I begged him—but he refused. His face became pale when I told him that I knew about an indiscretion of his—and that I would send a letter revealing it to a certain person. Reluctantly he agreed—but he needed some chemicals and equipment from his laboratory.

It was after seven o'clock when Alan returned to the library to inform me he had done what he was asked to do—and he hoped we would never see each other again.

By eight-thirty, exquisitely dressed and wearing a buttonhole of Parma violets, I was ushered into Lady Marborough's living room. For a moment I keenly felt the terrible pleasure of a double life.

But a fear ever haunted me. Sometimes at a dinner party I would leave suddenly and rush back to town to see that the door had not been tampered with and that the picture was still there. What if it should be stolen? The very thought of it made me cold with terror. The world would then know my secret.

One summer evening, while sitting in the library, I felt a wild longing for the unstained purity of my childhood. I felt repentant for my evil passions—and sorry to learn that Alan Campbell had committed suicide. A new life. That was what I wanted. If my life became pure, perhaps every sign of evil would be expelled from the picture. Perhaps even now with such repentant thoughts, those horrible lines of passion would be gone. I had to see it again.

I quickly reached the attic room and pushed aside the purple hanging from the portrait. I cried out in pain.

"Oh! It did not change. The thing is still loathsome. What are those scarlet spots on my hand? It's blood. Blood newly spilt. Alan Campbell's blood.

"Why did I keep the picture so long? Everytime I think of it I am filled with terror—with fear that other eyes shall look upon it. I will destroy it.

"Here is the knife. I cleaned it many times so no stain would show. This knife killed Basil Hallward. It will now kill his work. I will kill the past and be free!"

A cry was heard and a crash. It was a quarter of an hour later before the coachman and footmen crept upstairs. They knocked but there was no reply. After vainly trying the door, they got on the roof, dropped on to a balcony and entered through a window.

Hanging upon the wall was a splendid portrait of their master as they had last seen him. Lying on the floor was a dead man, in evening dress, with a knife in his heart. He was withered, wrinkled, and loathsome to behold. It was not till they had examined the rings on his hands that they recognized who it was.

MADAME LOISEL

From *The Diamond Necklace*

The famous French story-teller, Guy de Maupassant, has been widely read for almost a century. This particular tale is one to be remembered because of its ironic ending. The setting is Paris.

Madame Matilda Loisel describes herself in the following manner:

I was one of those pretty, charming young ladies, born as if through an error of destiny, into a family of clerks. I had no dowry, no hopes of becoming known, appreciated, loved, or married to a man either rich or distinguished. So I allowed myself to marry a petty clerk in the office of the Board of Education.

I was unhappy, feeling that I was born for all delicacies and luxuries. The poverty of our apartment with its shabby walls and worn furniture annoyed me. I dreamed of opulent rooms with oriental hangings lighted by high bronze torches, with two footmen to carry out my every whim.

When we seated ourselves to dinner, before the

Madame Loisel

round table on which the cloth had been used for three days, my husband would uncover the tureen and exclaim with delight: "Oh! the good potpie!" while I would long for elegant dinners with shining silver, exquisite food and sparkling wine.

One evening my husband returned home with more elation than usual as he handed me a large envelope and asked me to read the card inside. It was an invitation to attend a social function to be held at a prominent residence.

My husband expected me to be delighted by such news. I said to him: "What do I want with that? What would I wear to such a fashionable affair? I have no dress that is suitable." I wept. He was grieved by my tears and asked how much a suitable gown would cost.

"I cannot tell exactly, but four hundred francs ought to cover it."

He turned a little pale but replied that he would give me the money.

The day before the ball arrived and my dress was nearly ready. Yet my mood was a disturbed one. When my husband questioned me about it, I said: "I am vexed not to have a jewel—not one stone—to adorn myself with. I shall have such a poverty-laden look that I would prefer not to go to the party."

He suggested that I wear some natural flowers. Three roses could be bought for ten francs, but I was not convinced. Then he recalled my rich friend, Madame Forestier. Why didn't I ask her to lend me some jewels.

I was delighted with the idea and the next day called at her house. She opened her large jewel case and said I should choose. I tried on bracelets, a collar of pearls, and a Venetian cross of gold. Then I discovered a superb necklace of diamonds. My heart skipped joyfully as I placed them about my throat.

"Could you lend me this? Only this?" I asked eagerly. My friend readily agreed.

That evening we attended the ball, and although it sounds boastful, I was certain that I was the prettiest of all the ladies present. I felt elegant and vivacious. All the men noticed me and wished to be presented. Every member of the cabinet asked to waltz with me. As I danced I was enwrapped in a cloud of happiness which is so sweet to the heart of a woman. All too soon the last strains were wafted away.

It was almost four o'clock when we returned home, after walking part of the way until a carriage was available. Hurriedly I removed my shabby wrap and stood before the mirror. I had to have one last glance at myself in my new glory. But my smile faded as I saw my reflection. The radiance was gone. I gasped.

"Oh! It's—it's gone! Madame Forestier's necklace!"

Hastily we looked in the folds of my dress, in the pockets of my wrap, but it was not there. I was positive I was still wearing it when we left the party.

Perhaps I had lost it in the street or in the carriage.

Madame Loisel

My husband went in search for it while I paced back and forth. It was near seven o'clock when my husband returned. He had found nothing. He had gone to the police and to the cab office. An advertisement was put in the newspapers offering a reward.

The day went by and no word. We decided to write a note to my friend, Madame Forestier, that the clasp of the necklace was broken and it was to be repaired. That would give us more time for it to be returned. But the week went by and we lost all hope. We were dreadfully aware that the necklace had to be replaced.

We had to visit several jewelers before we found a necklace which seemed exactly like the one I had lost. It was valued at forty thousand francs. We could get it for thirty-six thousand. Eighteen thousand francs was all we had. My husband borrowed the rest. So the next day I took the necklace to Madame Forestier. Her tone was rather cool as she rebuked me for not returning it sooner.

For the next ten years we experienced the horrible life of necessity. We sent away the maid and moved into more humble lodgings. I learned the heavy cares of a household. All the odious work in the kitchen, washing soiled linen which I hung on a line to dry, and with basket on my arm I would go to the grocer's, the butcher's and haggle over the last sou.

Every month it was necessary to renew some notes and pay others. My husband worked evenings, putting books in order for some merchants. This inflicted sentence left an imprint not only on our bodies but our spirit also.

At the end of ten years we had repaid all our debts. I had become a stony-hard woman so typical of a poor household. My hair was no longer dressed with care, my hands were red from washing the floors many times from large pails of water. There was little evidence remaining of the beauty that I had once flaunted so proudly.

Then one Sunday afternoon I took a walk in the Champs Elysées, to forget for awhile the cares of the week. Suddenly I saw a woman with a child approaching. It was Madame Forestier. She was still young and pretty. Should I speak to her? Yes, I would.

I approached her. "Good morning, Jeanne. I see you don't recognize me. Afraid I do look shabby and common. I am Matilda Loisel. Yes, I have changed. I didn't stay young and beautiful like you. We have had some miserable days since I last saw you—my husband and I—and all because of you. I mean, you recall that diamond necklace that you loaned me to wear to that ball? Well, I lost it that evening. Oh, of course I returned the necklace—but it was another, exactly like it. And it has taken us ten years to pay for it. Perhaps you can understand how difficult that was for us who had nothing. But we are now out of debt. All is paid and I am content.

"Yes, of course. We bought a diamond necklace to

Madame Loisel 73

replace yours. So now— What? Jeanne, what are you saying? Oh, *mon Dieu!* Those diamonds were false? Why didn't you say so when I came to borrow it? Five hundred francs. You say they were worth only five hundred francs. So we struggled ten years for that—lived little better than beggars—to pay off a debt of five hundred francs."

MR. WHITE

From *The Monkey's Paw*

This thriller by the British author, W.W. Jacobs, is long remembered for its suspenseful climax. It has also been adapted as an exciting one-act play.

The setting seems serene—a small, modestly-furnished house some miles away from the nearest city. The family group seated by the fireside conveys the mood for a peaceful evening. It includes Mr. White, an elderly, grey-bearded man—his wife—and their grown son, Herbert. The two men are playing a game of chess while the woman seems content with her knitting.

It seems impossible to imagine that an event would happen within a few hours which would soon bring tragedy into their lives.

Mr. White recalls that fatal evening.

If I could only forget it. Better yet, if it had only been a bad dream. But I remember it all too vividly.

I had made a few reckless moves on the board and was losing the game. Outside the wind and rain tried to outdo each other. It was beastly annoying. I had invited an old friend of mine, Sergeant-Major Morris for supper. It was to be his first visit to our home.

"I hardly think he'll come tonight. Listen how that wind is howling. And such beastly rain. That's the worst of living so far from town. This is such an out-of-the way place. And such a miserable road. Just because there're only two houses around is no excuse for that."

I had no sooner said that, when the front gate banged loudly and heavy footsteps were heard coming toward the door.

"There he is." I hurried to admit him.

Morris was a tall, burly man of ruddy complexion. I introduced him to my wife and son, and led him toward the fireside. Then I placed a small copper kettle on the fire, and got the whiskey and tumblers ready.

Sipping our drinks, we were entertained by the tales told by the old soldier. He had been in many distant places, seen strange people, and done fearless deeds.

"He had twenty-one years of that," I informed my wife and son. "I remember when he went away. We both worked in the warehouse. He was a slip of a youth then. Now, look at him.

"But you spoke of India. I'd like to go there myself. Just to look around a bit, you know. I should like to see those old temples and fakirs and jugglers.

And what was that you started to tell me the other day, Morris? Something about a paw?"

Morris wanted to dismiss it, but he did admit that it might be called magic. Then he set down his glass, fumbled in his pocket and revealed the article in his hand. "An ordinary little monkey's paw, dried to a mummy," he called it.

My wife drew back and shuddered. I reached out and examined it. "And what is there special about it?" I asked.

He told us a spell was put on it by an old fakir—a holy man who wanted to show that fate rules people's lives. Three men could each have three wishes from it. The first man had his three wishes, Morris said. The man's last wish was for death. That was how Morris got the paw, he explained.

"And did you have your three wishes?" I eagerly asked.

His face whitened, and with an unsteady hand he gulped the rest of his drink. Yes, his three wishes were granted.

"Well, if you've had your three wishes, it's no good to you now. Why do you keep it?"

It was just a fancy, he imagined. He had an idea to sell the paw but realized most people would doubt its magic. Besides it had caused enough mischief already. He took the paw from me, glanced at it gravely, and then flung it upon the fire. I quickly

Mr. White

stooped down and snatched it away. I ignored his plea that I let it burn.

"If you don't want it, Morris, give it to me."

Morris urged me to throw it back, but I shook my head.

"How do you do it—when you want to make a wish?"

He told me to hold it up in my right hand and wish aloud—but warned me of the consequences. I smiled as I put the talisman in my pocket. Then I placed chairs around the table and motioned to my friend to join us for supper.

During the meal and afterward we all sat enthralled as Morris recalled his adventures in India. All too soon it was time for him to catch the last train back to the city.

Herbert remembered the monkey's paw, and jokingly said we now could be rich, famous, and happy. Why didn't I wish to be an emperor? Then I couldn't be henpecked. My wife made some good-natured remark to that.

I took the paw from my pocket. "I don't know what to wish for, and that's a fact. It seems to me I've got all I want."

Herbert reminded me of the debt we owed on the house. Two hundred pounds would clear it. We'd be very happy if we could free ourselves of that obligation. Why didn't I wish for that?

I held up the paw in my right hand and said clearly, "I wish for two hundred pounds." Then I shivered as it fell from my hand.

"It—it moved! As I wished it twisted in my hand like a snake."

My wife thought I imagined it. On his way to bed, Herbert bade us good night and added with a grin, that the money would be tied up in a big bag in the middle of my bed.

But the next morning with the wintry sun streaming over our breakfast table, what had happened last evening seemed like a fantastic yarn. How could that dirty, shriveled paw on the sideboard have magic powers? However, my wife and son did mention it again. How could we believe such nonsense? she said. Herbert warned me to be careful. The two hundred pounds might drop on my head from the sky.

"Morris said the things happen so naturally that you might call it a coincidence," I recalled.

Then with a few merry remarks, Herbert left for work. But I still insisted that the paw had moved in my hand.

After we had our noonday meal, I noticed my wife standing by the window and looking out for a longer time than usual.

"What's the matter?" I asked, and crossed to her side. A strange, well-dressed man stood in front of our gate. He seemed to hesitate about coming in. Then he decided to do so.

Mr. White

My wife hurriedly unfastened her apron before she opened the door to admit him. He was hesitant before he told us the reason for his call. Then he explained that he was from Maw and Meggins. That was the firm which employed Herbert. Alarmed, my wife asked if anything had happened to Herbert.

"There, there, Mother. Sit down, and don't jump to conclusions. I'm sure this gentleman isn't here to bring us bad news."

In a low voice the caller told us that Herbert had been hurt. While doing his work he was caught in the machinery. It had crushed the life out of him.

I stared blankly out the window. Herbert was the only child we had. How could we live on without him?

Then the man said that the firm sent their sympathy. They also disclaimed all responsibility in the accident. But in consideration of our son's service, they wished to present a certain sum as compensation.

I glanced at the visitor with a look of horror. "How —how much?" I asked.

"Two hundred pounds," he replied.

We buried Herbert in a cemetery two miles away. Our grief was almost too heavy for two old hearts to bear. A lonely week went by.

I awoke one night to find my wife weeping by the window.

"Come back to bed," I said. "You will be cold."

But she kept on weeping. It was colder for our son, she said. Then a few minutes later she awoke me with a start.

"What is it? What's the matter?" I asked.

She spoke wildly about the monkey's paw.

"But why do you want it? It's downstairs in the parlor. What do you mean—why didn't I think of it before?"

She reminded me of the other two wishes.

"But we had one. Wasn't that enough?"

She was almost hysterical. I was to wish for our boy to be alive again.

"No, I can't do it. You are mad. Our first wish was granted—but that was a coincidence. Our son is at peace in the cemetery. How can we wish him to be alive again?"

But she screamed on and insisted that I get the monkey's paw.

In the darkness I felt my way to the parlor. There on the mantelpiece was the cursed thing. My brow was cold with sweat as I returned to the bedroom. My wife commanded me to make the wish.

"This is foolish and wicked," I said.

But she repeated the words, "Wish. Wish. Wish."

My voice quivered and my hand trembled as I raised it. "I wish my son alive again." The thing throbbed and fell from my hand.

I sank into a chair. My wife walked to the window and raised the blind. The candle was burning low and

Mr. White

threw flickering shadows on the ceiling and walls, then it sputtered out. We waited. It was with a sense of relief that I realized the paw had failed. I crept back to bed and a few minutes later my wife returned silently beside me.

We didn't speak but listened to the ticking of the clock. A stair creaked and a mouse scurried noisely through the wall. The darkness seemed to crush down upon me. I arose, struck a match, and went downstairs for a candle.

At the foot of the stairs the match went out. Then I heard a faint knock at the door. The match fell from my hand. I stood motionless. Again I heard the knock. It was a little louder. A third knock sounded through the house.

My wife appeared at the top of the stairs and asked what was that noise.

"It's a rat. It passed me on the stairs. Go back to bed."

But the knock was repeated.

She ran down the steps but I caught her by the arm. "What are you going to do?" I asked.

She struggled and cried out that Herbert was at the door. She forgot that the cemetery was two miles away. He couldn't be here sooner. She had to open the door.

"For God's sake, don't let him in. Herbert has been dead a week. What will he look like? We can't let him in!"

But she broke free and ran toward the door. She struggled to reach the bolt—it was too high for her. She begged me to open the door.

It had to be done. There was one wish left. Could I do it in time? I returned quickly to the bedroom and on my hands and knees groped wildly for the paw. I heard the scraping of a chair as my wife put it in front of the door so she could unlock it. Then I heard the creaking of the bolt.

"Oh, God, let me find it!" I called out. Then my hand found it. I held it up and gasped, "I wish my son to return to his grave."

The knocking stopped suddenly. I hurried downstairs just as the door opened and a blast of cold wind swept through the room. There was no one at the door. My wife wailed with misery. We looked out toward the gate. Only the street lamp flickered and shone on a quiet and deserted road.

MRS. McWILLIAMS

From *Mrs. McWilliams and the Lightning*

Mark Twain had the special gift for injecting infectious humor in his writings. His penetrating insight into the foibles and follies of human nature produced many chuckles for his readers.

Evangeline McWilliams, a farmer's wife, had a quaking fear of thunderstorms. One night she was rudely awakened from her slumber by such a disturbance.

It is true what Mortimer, my husband, says about my affliction. He says that I can face a mouse, or the very devil himself—but I go all to pieces at the first flash of lightning.

So on that particular night, a clap of thunder woke me up. I scampered out of bed and ran to the boot closet. Trembling I called out:

"Mortimer! Mortimer! I am here—shut up in the boot closet. You ought to be ashamed to lie there and sleep so, with such an awful storm going on. Come out of that bed instantly. I should think you would take some care of your life, for my sake and the children's, if not for your own.

"Don't talk to me, Mortimer. You know there is no place so dangerous as a bed in such a thunderstorm as this. All the books say that. Yet there you would lie and deliberately throw away your life—for goodness knows what, unless for the sake of arguing and—"

Mortimer got out of bed—but he had to swear to do it. Then a glare of lightning flashed again and an awful blast of thunder.

"Oh! There! You see the result. Oh, Mortimer, how can you be so profligate as to swear at such a time as this? I don't see how you can act so, when you know there is not a lightning rod on the place—and your poor wife and children are absolutely at the mercy of Providence.

"What are you doing? Lighting a match at such a time as this! Are you stark mad? Put it out! Put it out instantly! Are you determined to sacrifice us all? You know there is nothing attracts lightning like a light."

Then we heard another clap of thunder.

"Oh! Now you see what you've done! Mortimer, did you say your prayers tonight? Don't make any excuses. How could you neglect such a thing at such a time as this?"

And then, as if it was the devil's doing, another crash of thunder.

"Oh dear, dear, dear! I know it struck something.

We never shall see the light of another day. When we are gone, you can remember that it was your dreadful language that—

"Mortimer! Your voice sounds as if— Mortimer, are you actually standing in front of that open fireplace?

"Get away from it this moment! You do seem determined to bring destruction on us all. Don't you know that there is no better conductor for lightning than an open chimney? Now where have you got to?

"Oh, for pity's sake! Have you lost your mind? Move away from that window this moment! The very children in arms know it is fatal to stand near a window in a thunderstorm. Dear, dear, I know I shall never see the light of another day.

"Mortimer, what is that rustling? What are you doing? Oh, Mortimer, you can't put on those pantaloons. Throw those things away. I do believe you would deliberately put on those clothes when you know perfectly well that all authorities agree that woolen stuffs attract lightning.

"And don't sing! What can you be thinking of? If I told you once, I have told you a hundred times that singing causes vibrations in the atmosphere which interrupt the flow of the electric fluid, and—

"What on earth are you opening the door for? No harm in it? There's death in it. Anybody that has given this subject any attention knows that to create a draught is to invite the lightning. You haven't half shut it. Shut it tight—and do hurry, or we are all destroyed. Oh, it is an awful thing to be shut up with a lunatic at such a time as this.

"Mortimer, what are you doing? Are you turning on the water? Mortimer, you have certainly parted with the remnant of your mind! When lightning strikes any other substance once, it strikes water fifty times. Do turn it off.

"Oh dear, I am sure that nothing in the world can save us. It does seem to me that—

"Mortimer, what was that? You knocked a picture down. Then you are too close to the wall! I never heard of such imprudence! Don't you know that there's no better conductor for lightning than a wall? Come away from there! And you came as near as anything to swearing, too. Oh, how can you be so desperately wicked, and your family in such peril?

"Mortimer, did you order a feather bed, as I asked you to do? Forgot it! It may cost you your life. If you had a feather bed now and could spread it in the middle of the room and lie on it, you would be perfectly safe.

"Something must be done for your preservation. Give me that German book that is on the mantlepiece and a candle. Don't light it. Give me a match and I will light it in here. That book has some directions in it.

"Mortimer, what was that? The cat! Oh, destruction! Catch her and shut her up in the washstand. Do be quick, love, cats are full of electricity. I just know my hair will turn white with this night's awful perils.

"It says in this book that the safest thing is to stand on a chair in the middle of the room. The legs of the chair must be insulated with non-conductors. That is, you must set the legs of the chair in glass tumblers.

"Oh! Hear that? Do hurry, Mortimer, before you are struck.

"And then it says—but this German seems a little mixed. I am not sure if it means that you must keep metals *about* you or keep them *away* from you. But I believe metal is sort of a lightning rod, so it should be about you. Put on your fireman's helmet, Mortimer—that is mostly metal.

"And now I think your middle ought to be protected. Buckle on your militia saber, please. And you ought to have some way to protect your feet. Do please, put on your spurs.

"Mortimer, it says in this book—but I am not sure if it means that it is dangerous to ring the church bell during a thunderstorm. But perhaps one should ring some sort of bell. That might scare the storm away. So we don't want to waste precious time to talk. Get the large dinner bell. It is right there in the hall. Quick, Mortimer dear. I do believe we are going to be saved at last!

"There, you have the bell. Now climb on the chair, dear, and ring it loud."

Mortimer muttered something, some swear words

probably, then stood on the chair and rang the bell. He was wearing his night dress, the fireman's helmet, saber, and spurs on his feet. After ringing the bell for about five minutes, he wanted to stop.

"Keep on ringing it, Mortimer. I believe it is saving us. The lightning and thunder have stopped."

Then I saw a sight that made me scream.

"Oh! Look—look, Mortimer. Our shutters are opening! What—what is doing that? Why, it's our neighbor, Mr. Gadsby. And there is Mr. Thompkins, too."

Mercy, if the two men didn't hold up their lanterns and peer in the window. When they saw Mortimer they said they had heard the bell and asked what was the matter.

Poor Mortimer, I guess he felt foolish as he stepped down from the chair, holding the bell and dressed so strangely. He sort of stammered that because of the thunderstorm he was trying to keep off the lightning. The two men looked surprised at that —and when they burst out laughing, I thought they were plumb out of their minds. It was a beautiful starlight night, they said. Then Mr. Thompkins, wiping his eyes from so much laughing, tried to explain what had happened.

"Mortimer, what did he say? The thunder we heard came from a cannon? Mercy. But we saw the lightning. Oh, that was from the cannon too? Well, for pity's sake, why do they have to wake up folk when it is past midnight? Oh, it was news from the telegraph. And what was so important that it cannot wait until morning? Oh. So Garfield was nominated for president."

So there was the reason for that peculiar thunderstorm. You might say it cured me of complaining about them—in front of Mortimer, I mean. Because if I did, he would swear a string of words that would shame the devil.

"DOC" SILVERTON

From *To Make a Hoosier Holiday*

George Ade wrote for "the family trade," as he called it. He was born and died in Indiana, although he did travel extensively during his lifetime. He was hailed as a journalist, columnist, humorist, and a playwright, aside from his skill as a writer of short stories.

This one has a small-town, sarsaparilla-soda flavor and "Doc" can tell us about the activities that go on there.

If you try to find our town on the state map of Indiana, it's only a black dot. It is called Musselwhite.

The train passes through early in the mornin'. An' from a parlor car you can see a brindle-colored depot, a few brick stores, an' a stragglin' row of frame houses. The horses at the hitch rack look more alert than the few sleepy lookin' people on the platform. A stranger goin' through would never think of Musselwhite again.

We have three churches. The Catholic one is at the other end of town. Near the general store is the

Zion Methodist—an' across the street from it, the Campbellites.

Now these two wings of the Protestant faith do not always flap in unison. You couldn't call it petty rivalry between the two flocks. It's jes' a strong an' healthy competition, that's what it is—each strivin' to pick in the vineyard the larger bunch of grapes.

If the Zion church—I belong to that one—gives a mush-an'-milk sociable—then the Campbellites announce a rummage party. The Campbellites have their Sunday-school in the mornin' right before the regular service—while the Methodists have theirs in the afternoon. But you always hear which one had the largest attendance—an' the most money in the collection plate. Children can attend both services —while their parents can skip one of 'em an' stay home an' read the Sunday papers.

A few years ago we were in an awful fix about what to do about Christmas Eve. Each church always has a program for that night. How can a child be in both places at the same time? Most of 'em go to the one which has the most spectacular entertainment—an' gives the larger box of mixed candy. Just an ordinary Christmas tree with strings of popcorn an' candles no longer satisfy the little ones. They want to see Santy Claus in a fur coat, want to sing in cantatas, or speak pieces dressed up as shepherds or wise men or angels.

One time the Campbellites gave a program an'

when Kris Kringle came through the fireplace an' said, "Is this the town of Musselwhite?"—little Tad Saulsbury piped up, "I know who it is. It's Jake Francis."

So we Methodists had to plan something diff'rent. We had a committee meetin' in November in my office. Sam Woodson an' Orville Hufty were present.

I said: "Boys, I heard them Campbellites are goin' to give another chimney-corner show. So we got to do somethin' to offset it. I claim that the Christmas tree is played out. Since they're startin' to ship in these evergreen trees from Chicago, a good many people have their own trees right at home.

"That's right, Orville. We got to give 'em somethin' that ain't been done before. So if you'll help me with a little scheme, we can beat 'em at their own game. I've been layin' awake nights an' thinkin' about it. Now don't laugh when I tell you. It's nothin' more or less than a weddin'.

"That's it exactly, Sam. We get somebody married on Christmas Eve."

"Sure, people get married every day. But not the people that I'm thinkin' about. Can you imagine what kind of a crowd we'd have in our church if we advertise that old 'Baz' Leonard is goin' to get married to Miss Wheatley?

"Go ahead. Take your time to get over that one. Sure 'Baz' is goin' to marry her. Only he don't know it—yet. He likes nothin' better than to show off in public. So what better chance than this? An' that Miss Wheatley—she is long overdue to get married to someone.

"Nope, it can't be anybody else. 'Baz' is the man. If we got a public character in this town it's 'Baz' Leonard. An' if there's a woman in town that's supposed to be out of the marryin' class, it's Beulah Wheatley. Her gettin' married to anyone would be about the biggest piece of news you could spring on Musselwhite. But her gettin' married to 'Baz' Leonard! Say! They won't have a handful of people at their chimney-corner show.

"Why boys, it's the simplest thing in the world. All we do is to announce that we're goin' to give Miss Wheatley a Christmas present.

"Now I've thought it all out. We'll have Santy Claus bring in the marriage license an' present it to 'Baz.' Then we'll lead the happy couple to the altar. And after that Brother King will do a scientific job of splicin'. Then we'll give 'em their combination Christmas an' weddin' presents. The diff'rent Sunday-school classes can chip in an' buy presents. They'll be glad to do it.

"Jes' leave it to me. I guarantee to have 'Baz' on hand when the time comes. What I want you fellas to do is have the women go after Miss Wheatley. We must take it for granted that they're already engaged. So have the women go over an' congratulate her. An' after that, have them convince her that if she has a church weddin' she'll get a raft of presents."

An' so the very next day it started. The story jumped from house to house—across farm lots—over ditches—through the deep woods until it was talked about as far away as Burdette's Grove. There was a piece about it in our weekly newspaper, *The Courier*. "The couple will be united in the holy bonds of wedlock," it said.

But I think you should know a little more about the bride an' groom to be. As I mentioned earlier, if there was a crowd around, "Baz" did his best to be noticed. He was a member of the Volunteer Fire Department—an' every time there was a parade, he would beat the dickens out of the bass drum. Whenever a travelin' magician or hypnotist would give a show an' ask for "someone from the audience to kindly step upon the stage," it was "Baz" who always went up. He was a constable whenever they needed one —an' every summer would go off to a soldiers' reunion some place. It seemed he was happiest when he was up there on a pedestal an' looked at. His front name is Ballantyne—but he didn't brag about that. He lived in a small frame house that was covered more by a mortgage than by paint.

As for Miss Beulah Wheatley—she was a small, prim, maiden lady who looked out at the world through a pair of bull's-eye spectacles. When it came to church activities, she was a reg'lar Joan of Arc— doin' all she could for foreign missionary work. She owned the house she lived in—an' it was said she had invested some money.

As you can guess, no two people in Musselwhite were more surprised by the engagement than Mr. "Baz" Leonard and Miss Beulah Wheatley.

The first chance that I had, I called him in my office an' gave him a long an' violent handshake.

"Well, I'll be jiggered, 'Baz'. It's somethin' you ought to have done years ago. She's a fine woman, an' she's got a little property, an' I don't see how you could do better."

Then he said somethin' about not havin' seen Miss Wheatley for about six weeks—an' then they didn't talk about nothin' except the Plymouth Rock chickens she had bought.

I patted him on the shoulder. "You scalawag. You kept it quiet as long as you could. Why, Miss Wheatley is so proud of gettin' you away from all those widows around town. So you can't blame her for braggin' a little. An' now that it's all settled we're goin' to give you the biggest weddin' that was ever seen in this neck of the woods."

Then I clinched the whole deal by givin' a supper at the Commercial Hotel. There was "Baz" an' Miss Wheatley, lookin' sorta bewildered at each other across the celery tops. But with all them witnesses present, how could they have the courage to arise an' protest?

Then a day or so later, word come to the committee that the groom was weakenin'. The prospect of a straight an' narrow matrimony with a small but determined woman did not tickle him pink or any other color. I met "Baz" in front of the post office later on, an' right away he told me we'd have to call it off.

"You can't call it off, 'Baz.' How could you ever explain—when your engagement was announced in front of all those witnesses?

"Sure, I announced it. But you was present—an' silence gives consent, don't it? If you try to back out now, she can sue you for breach of promise. Why, I'm surprised at you. After all your friends have done for you in this thing.

"Oh. So you ain't got any clothes that's fit to wear, huh? Well, I 'spect we could see that you got a new suit."

So that Christmas Eve came. Musselwhite was keyed up to a high pitch of glad expectation. An' as for all the people who came to our church that night —we had to squeeze 'em in. Miss Wheatley, all in white, with smellin' salts an' six married women to give her courage, waited in the pastor's study.

But where was the groom? Where was that grizzled veteran who had faced death on many fields of battle? Layin' on his bed in his new suit, tellin' us, the committee, who was present—that he was at death's door an' there could be no weddin'.

"Where does it hurt you?" I asked. "Your pulse is all right and you got a good color."

Then I said to Sam an' Orville, as I rolled up my

sleeves. "There's nothin' the matter with 'Baz' except that he's a little overheated by the pleasure of this gladsome occasion. I'll bleed him. That will cool him off an' he'll be O.K."

Then I took out a long knife from my case. Well, that did it. "Baz" sat up an' showed immediate improvement.

"Now you quit this tomfoolin' an' come along with us. We ain't got a minute to spare."

"Baz" stood up with a deep sigh an' we bundled him into his overcoat. We lead him toward the church. In front of the Gridley house "Baz" stopped.

"What's the matter now, 'Baz'? Oh, you need a drink of water. Well, you can get one at the church."

But what does he do but insist that the water from the Gridley well was the best in town. So we waited at the front gate—but "Baz" didn't come back. We looked around.

"He couldn't get away so soon," I said. "There ain't any tracks in the snow. Why—I'll be jiggered! Look up there—up in that cherry tree. Come on down from there, 'Baz'. You're actin' like a child. I didn't think an old soldier like you would be scared to face a crowd of people."

We all coaxed him to come down from the tree—but "Baz" shouted back that it was a put-up job.

So I finally said, "Go over to the church, Sam, an' tell the whole crowd to come here an' look at the bridegroom that's gone to roost like a chicken."

Well, that brought him down. He didn't want no

crowd around to see him like that. So we led him away—like a lamb to the slaughter.

People in Musselwhite said it was the makin' of "Baz" Leonard. His habits did improve, 'cause he had a wife who made him walk the chalk line. He now lives in a cottage that is spic an' span. So he should be happy. But sometimes at a Sunday mornin' service, when "Baz" looks across at me—his eyes seem to say, "You rascal. You did this to me."

After that Christmas Eve I never had any more bright ideas for makin' it a special holiday.

MISS CANDACE WHITCOMB

From *The Village Singer*

Mary E. Wilkins Freeman, author of this story, was praised by Henry James for her "comedy and elegy of the realities of rustic New England."

For the past forty years, Miss Whitcomb, a tall, slender spinster, was the soprano soloist on the church choir. Little had she suspected that her solo on that particular Sunday would be the last one she would render there.

The following took place in the parlor of Miss Whitcomb during those 1890 years. We will allow her to relate what had happened to bring about such a turn of events.

It all started on a Thursday evenin' about eight o'clock, when the choir come here. They pretended it was a nice little surprise. They brought cookies an' oranges, an' was jest as nice as they could be, an' I was real tickled. I never had a surprise party before in my life. Jenny Carr played on the parlor organ over there, an' they wanted me to sing alone, an' I never suspected a thing. I've been mad ever since to think what a fool I was, an' how they must have laughed in their sleeves.

When they'd gone, I found this photograph album on the table. It was all done up as nice as you please, an' directed to Miss Candace Whitcomb from her many friends. I opened it an' there was the letter inside givin' me notice to quit.

If they'd gone about it any decent way, told me right out an' honest that they'd got tired of me, an' wanted Alma Way to sing instead of me, I wouldn't have minded so much. They said in the letter that they'd always set great value on my services, an' it wasn't from any lack of appreciation that they turned me off. They thought the duty was gettin' a little too arduous for me. Hm! I hadn't complained.

If they'd turned me right out an' said, "Here, you get out," but instead they spill molasses, as it were, all over the threshold, tryin' to make me think it's all so nice an' sweet.

My cottage sets close to the south side of the church. So the next Sunday mornin' I stayed at home. An' bein' very warm even for May, I opened the window an' could hear the singin' real good from the church. I set down to my organ, an' waited for Alma Way's solo. When it begun, I sang out a hymn as loud as I could, an' did all the verses, too.

Well, it didn't surprise me none when that afternoon who should open my gate an' come up the walk but Mr. Pollard, our minister. When he rang the door bell I answered, but I jest kept lookin' mad.

"Good mornin'," I said, an' returned to my chair by the window. I didn't ask him to come in, but he did, set himself on the rockin' chair, an' wiped his face. Then he spoke about what a pleasant day it was—an' how beautiful the lilacs were in a pitcher on the parlor organ. Then he come to the point, an' said that my singin' so loud had disturbed 'em in church, an' that he hoped I wasn't hurt that he spoke about it.

I kept lookin' out the window, as I said, "I ain't disturbed at it. I did it on purpose.

"You needn't look at me like that, Mr. Pollard. I know jest what I'm about. I sang the way I did on purpose, an' I'm goin' to do it again, an' I'd like to see you stop me. I guess I've got a right to set down to my own organ, an' sing a psalm tune on a Sabbath day, if I want to. There ain't no amount of palaverin' a-goin' to stop me.

"Look at that!" I said, an' swung aside my skirts a little. My feet was restin' on that large, red-plush photograph album. "It makes a nice footstool, don't it?

"I know what you're a-goin' to say, Mr. Pollard, an' now I'm goin' to have my way. I want to know what you think of folks that pretend to be Christians treatin' anybody the way they've treated me. Here I've sung in those singin' seats forty years. I ain't never missed a Sunday except when I've been sick, an' many a time I sung when I'd better been in bed. An' now I'm turned out without a word of warnin'.

"My voice is jest as good as it ever was; there can't anybody say it ain't. It wa'n't ever quite so high-pitched as that Way's girl mebbe, but she flats an awful lot.

"S'pose they should turn you off, Mr. Pollard—come an' give you a photograph album, an' tell you to clear out. How'd you like it? I ain't findin' fault with your preachin'. It was always good enough to suit me. But perhaps folks ain't so took up with your sermons as when you was a young man.

"An' there's William Emmons, too. He's three years older'n I am, even if he does lead the choir an' run all the singin' in town. If my voice has given out, it stands to reason his has. It ain't though. William Emmons sings jest as well as he ever did.

"Why don't they turn him out the way like they did me, an' give him a photograph album? Mebbe it would be a good idea to send everybody as soon as they get a little old, onto some desert island an' give 'em each a photograph album. Then they can set down an' look at pictures the rest of their days. Mebbe the government will take it up.

"Then they come here last Thursday evenin', so sweet as sugar cake, an' leave that present. I'd sent the album back had I known who started it. So I'm usin' it for a footstool. That's all it's good for, 'cordin'

Miss Candace Whitcomb 103

to my way of thinkin'. An' I ain't even particular to get the dust off my shoes before I use it, neither.

"I've made up my mind that I'm goin' to sing Sundays the way I did this mornin', an' I don't care what folks say. I want 'em to know that I ain't trod down quite flat—that there's a little rise left in me. I got a right to play a psalm tune an' sing. If you don't like it, you can move the meetin' place."

Well, the minister jest set there an' stared, an' looked a little helpless. Then he said we should kneel an' ask guidance of the Lord.

But I didn't do it. "I don't see any use prayin' about it. I don't think the Lord got much to do with it, anyhow."

By then it was about time for the afternoon service, so Mr. Pollard went on his way. I stayed at the window an' watched the folks pass by an' heard the church bell ring. Then I set in front of the organ, arranged my singin' book, an' waited. Alma Way had jest sang a note or two, when I played an' sang like fury.

After the church meetin' was done, as I went over to my chair by the window, my knees felt weak. I heard a slam of the gate, an' my nephew, Wilson Ford, rushed into the parlor. He was engaged to Alma Way, if you ain't heard about it. Well, he was boilin' mad an' asks if I was crazy, an' that he would pitch the organ out the window. After that, he said, he would board up the window to shut off my singin'.

That didn't help my temper none, so I yelled back at him. "This ain't your house, an' it won't never be. I ain't bound to give any reason to a young fella like you. But I'll tell you one thing, Wilson Ford—after the way you spoke today, you shan't never have one cent of my money. An' you can't never marry that Way girl if you don't have this house, 'cause you can't take her to live with your mother. I'm goin' to make another will, an' you won't get a cent of my money, nor your mother, neither. Now I wish you'd go home. I want to lay down. I'm 'bout sick."

At seven o'clock that evenin' the meetin' bell rang again, but I had shut the parlor organ, an' went to bed. The doctor was called in, an' my sister, Nancy, nursed me. I knew that it wa'n't long for me to live.

The next Sunday mornin' I asked that the minister see me. He prayed with me, an' I asked for his forgiveness. "I hadn't ought to—to spoke so," I said. "I was—dreadful wrought up."

After he went, I said to my sister,"Nancy, I wish you'd go out, when the meetin's done, an' head off Alma an' Wilson. Ask 'em to come in. I feel as if—I'd like to hear her sing."

When they come, I smiled to 'em, an' said to my nephew: "Wilson, I ain't altered that will. You an' Alma can come here an' live—when I'm gone. Alma can have all my things."

Then I spoke to Alma: "I thought mebbe you'd be

willin' to—to sing for me. That psalm tune, *Jesus, Lover of My Soul,* would be nice."

She sang two verses. I looked at her an' said weakly, "You were a little flat on—*soul.*"

PERKINS OF PORTLAND

From *The Adventure of the Crimson Cord*

Ellis Parker Butler is best known for his story entitled Pigs is Pigs, *which had a tremendous circulation.*

However, his Perkins is such a clever promoter that he deserves our attention. With his persuasive manner he would feel right at home with the peddlers on Madison Avenue.

If I do say it myself, I am the greatest schemer in or out of Chicago. You may call me a genius, if you like—or I will answer to Perkins the Great—Perkins the Originator—or the Great and Only Perkins of Portland.

One day I walked into the office of a friend of mine. He looked gloomy, and said he was tired of sitting there with nothing to do but clip coupons from his bonds. He wanted some excitement—an adventure. He was sick of his old cash and wanted to make some new, up-to-date cash—but he had no scheme.

Pushing back my hat, and rubbing my hands together with relish, I said: "My boy, there are millions of schemes. You've thousands of 'em right here in your office. You're falling over them, sitting on them, walking on them. Schemes? Everything is a scheme. Everything has money in it!

"But why delay? Time is money. Hand me something from your desk."

He handed me a ball of string. I looked at it with great admiration. "What is this? Oh, you say it's a ball of red twine. Ah, that's the difference between mediocrity and genius! Mediocrity always sees red twine. Genius sees a ball of crimson cord!"

Then I snipped off a few pieces of it with a scissors. "The Crimson Cord! What does it suggest? There, that's mediocrity again. To you it suggests a parcel from the druggist because he uses red twine. But to me it suggests mystery! Daggers! Murder! Strangling! Clues! The Crimson Cord—

"That's right, it sounds like a book. Great! A novel! *The* novel! Think of the words *A Crimson Cord* in blood-red letters six feet high on a white background."

Then I passed my hat over my eyes and shuddered so he would get the effect. "The cover of the book will be white—virgin, spotless white—with black lettering, and the cord in crimson. With each copy we'll give a crimson silk cord for a bookmark. Each copy will be done up in a white box and tied with crimson cord."

I closed my eyes and tilted my head upward. "It'll

be a thick book, with wide margins, and a gloomy foreword."

Then I opened my eyes, set my hat on straight, and moved toward the door. "I am now getting the contracts for advertising. We must boom *The Crimson Cord.* We must boom her big!"

So we took a full-page advertisement in every worthwhile magazine. Sometimes it appeared among the breakfast foods, and sometimes it was sandwiched in between the automobiles and the hot-water heaters. Only one publication placed it among the books.

I was so busy scheming all kinds of ways to bring the title before the public, that I was surprised when my friend reminded me that we still needed the novel. You know—the reading, the words.

I was stunned for only a moment. "Tut, tut! All in good time. The novel is easy. Anything will do. I'm no literary man myself. I don't read a book in a year."

My friend said he hadn't read a book in five years and knew nothing about them.

"Advertise. You can get anything from an apron to an ancestor if you advertise for it. Offer a prize— offer a thousand dollars for the best novel. There must be thousands of novels not in use."

So we advertised, and they came to us in basketsful and carloads. We had novels of all kinds— historical and hysterical, humorous and numerous, but particularly numerous. You'd be surprised to know how many ready-made novels can be had on short notice. It beats a quick lunch. And most of them are equally indigestible.

We were at a loss which one to pick. My friend read one or two of them and then gave up. I suggested that we draw lots for the one we should use. It really made little difference what the story was about. *The Crimson Cord* fits almost any kind of book. It could mean the guilt that bound two sinners —or the tie of affection that binds lovers—or a blood relationship—or it might be a mystification with nothing in the book about it.

One morning a manuscript arrived that was tied with a piece of red twine.

"This is it!" I shouted. "We will publish this book anonymously. We'll say that the only clue to the writer was the crimson cord that was tied around the manuscript."

My friend took care of the business deal with the author, a Miss Vincent, while I chased around other schemes.

On my next visit to the office, I brought along an armful of bundles which I spread on the desk.

"No, I didn't go to a bargain sale," I explained. "This is the aftermath! All it takes is genius. Else why Perkins the Great? Why not Perkins the Nobody?"

I picked an article from the pile. "Look at these

suspenders. Notice the red edge of the elastic." Then I selected another item. "See the red stripes on that tie. And those red laces on that pair of shoes. These things are all the aftermath. Those suspenders are the Crimson Cord suspenders. Those shoes are the Crimson Cord shoes. That tie is the Crimson Cord tie. Those crackers are the Crimson Cord brand. Perkins and Company gets out a great book. It sells five million copies. Dramatized, it runs three hundred nights. Everybody will talk Crimson Cord. Country goes Crimson Cord crazy. Result—up jump Crimson Cord this and Crimson Cord that.

"So what will we do? We will copyright the words Crimson Cord on a trademark for every possible thing, and get a ten percent royalty of all receipts."

On the first of October we announced in our advertisements that *The Crimson Cord* was a book. That it was the greatest novel of the century—a thrilling tale of love. That's what Miss Vincent, the author, said it was—a love story, and we took her word for it. We didn't bother to read it. The book was promised to the public by November first.

Then one day, Mr. Gilkowsky, the printer, called at the office and seemed agitated about something. He explained that the girl he was going with read all the trashy books and had read our manuscript. We didn't mind that. But when he told us that she read it before, and that it was published as a book by another author as *Lady Audley's Secret*, that gave us a jolt. Then we knew that Miss Vincent had flimflammed us. What she did was give us a typewritten copy of another novel.

It was a cinch that we couldn't publish *Lady Audley's Secret* as *The Crimson Cord*. All we could do about it was charge it off as profit and loss, and hustle around for another novel.

I thought Indiana was an honest state, so we put an advertisement in all the Indianapolis papers, and two days later we had ninety-eight historical novels. We picked one of the right length, sent it to Mr. Gilkowsky, and asked his sweetheart to read it. She had never read that one before. But to make sure, we sent a detective to Dillsville, Indiana, where the author lived, and his report was satisfactory.

So it was published and became an immense success. It was sold in every department store. Sometimes you found it next to Q & Z Corsets. We sold our first edition of five million copies within three months, got out an illustrated holiday edition, and even an edition de luxe.

With all the royalties from the aftermath and the profits on the book, we made —Well, I don't like to boast the exact hard cash. But for the pains of my genius, my friend has a cottage at Newport—and Perkins the Great has a country place at Lakewood.

MADAME KOLPAKOW

From *The Chorus Girl*

Anton Chekov is known primarily for his plays, which are still performed with success in many countries. For the reader he also contributed many short stories which involve Russian people in dramatic situations.

In a country house on one summer afternoon, a rendezvous was arranged between Nikolai Petrovitch Kolpakow and an actress named Pasha. It was interrupted by the appearance of a visitor—a young, beautiful lady, handsomely dressed in a refined style.

It was a difficult decision to reach, for me to pay a call and face that actress. I despised her. As a girl in the chorus, she was on display every night in the theatre. But I was desperate. She was responsible for a disgraceful dilemma. Perhaps I would have to beg for her help but she had to listen.

My fingers trembled as I rang the doorbell. I heard the sound of muffled voices—of a man and a woman. A few moments later the door opened and there she stood. I would have known she was an actress by her appearance. She had a voluptuous figure, painted cheeks, and bangs over her forehead. We stared at each other before she asked what I wished.

Without being invited, I entered the room and surveyed it. How commonplace it was. But one should not expect refinement from such a creature. I took a seat, then glanced at her, so she could observe that my eyes were red from crying.

"Is my husband here?" I asked. She looked frightened. That surprised me, as I expected an angry retort from such a question. "My husband, Nikolai Petrovitch Kolpakow—is he here?"

She denied knowing anyone by that name.

"You maintain then that he is not here? Yes, I am Madame Kolpakow. And you are a low, vulgar woman. I am very happy that I have finally a chance to tell you so face to face!

"It does not matter whether he is here or not. I came here to tell you shameful news. At my husband's place of business they discovered an embezzlement. They suspect Nikolai and are looking for him. They are going to arrest him."

Overcome with emotion, I rose and paced about the room. A moment later I was sobbing.

"Today he will be found and arrested. I know who led him on to all this. It was you. You low creature.

"I am powerless. But God sees everything! He is just! He will repay you for all my tears—all my sleepless nights!"

Again she denied knowing anything about him.

"You lie! I know everything. I know that there has not been a day during the last four months that he did not spend with you!

"He stole money from his office. For your sake he has committed a crime. But you cannot have principles, you who live only to wrong others. But I cannot believe that even you have lost your spark of humanity. He has a wife, he has children. If they sentence him and send him to Siberia, I and the children must starve. There remains one way to save us from misery and dishonor. If I can make good and deposit today nine hundred rubles, he will not be prosecuted.

"I do not beg of you nine hundred rubles. I ask for something entirely different. Men are in the habit of giving girls like you jewelry. Return to me the things my husband gave you!

"Oh, you deny that he gave you jewelry. Listen, I beg of you! I have been overcome by all this and called you unpleasant names. I beg you to forgive me. You must hate me. But if you are capable of pity, try to put yourself in my place. I implore you, give me back those things!"

Then she shrugged her shoulders and admitted Nikolai had given her two pieces of jewelry. She opened the drawer of her dresser and handed me a thin gold bracelet and a little ring with a red stone.

I was offended by such a pitiful contribution. "What are you giving me? I do not ask for alms, but for that which is not yours. I want what you induced my husband to give you.

"Thursday, when I met you with my husband on the Avenue, you wore expensive brooches and rings. You don't need to play for my benefit the part of an innocent lamb. For the last time I ask you, will you return those things to me or not?"

But the creature insisted those two pieces of jewelry were all he gave her. When she mentioned that he brought cake, I laughed shrilly.

"Cake. At home the children have nothing to bite and here you feast on cake. So you refuse to return to me those things?"

She seated herself in a rocking chair. I purposely waited to give her time to decide. Perhaps if I made a tearful last appeal she might relent. I pressed my handkerchief to my face.

"I beg of you, have pity. You have ruined my husband and wrecked his life. Yet it is you who can save him. Perhaps you feel no pity for him, but the children, think of them. Why should those innocent children suffer so?"

That plea seemed to touch her. She burst into tears. When she said that she had taken no financial advantages from Nikolai, I had to believe her. But I still insisted that she give me her jewelry.

"Give them to me. I am crying. I am lowering myself. If you wish me to do so, I will throw myself at your feet. Please! Please!"

I was willing to humiliate myself and kneel before her, if only to humiliate her even more. But before I could do so she arose. She consented to give me her jewelry, but insisted the things were not from Nikolai but from other gentlemen. Again she opened the drawer of her dresser. She handed me a diamond brooch, several rings and necklaces.

I examined the articles and spread them on the table. "This is not all. These things are not even worth five hundred rubles."

Then she screamed and told me to take everything and make myself rich. I made no reply but kept my gaze fixed on her, until she again went to the dresser. She threw a gold watch, a cigarette case, and a pair of cuff buttons on the table. There was no more, she assured me.

Without exchanging another word, I gathered up the things and walked out of the room.

When Nikolai returned home later that afternoon, he appeared remorseful. Although he never confessed it, I felt certain that he had heard everything from an adjoining room. When I deliberately mentioned Pasha, he interrupted and called her vile names. Then he reached for my hand and tenderly kissed it.

RANSIE BILBRO

From *The Whirligig of Life*

O. Henry lived in many sections of our country where he practised his keen insight of people by writings about them with deep understanding.

The locale of this story is a peaceful settlement near the Cumberland range in Tennessee, on a languid summer afternoon.

A cloud of dust is stirred up by a cart which clatters down the main street and stops before the office of the justice of the peace. Ransie Bilbro, a lean and tanned mountaineer and his wife, Ariela, who is dressed in faded calico, step from their rickety wagon and enter the dingy building. Ransie appears solemn as he explains the reason for their visit.

"Howdy. You be Benaja Widdup, justice o' the peace? So I reckon. That why we come here particlar —to see ya—me an' Ariela. She's my wife an' we—

"Come on in, Ariela. You bin a-hankerin' to come here. Come on, tell this—er—justice o' the peace what we come fer.

"That's right, Justice, we wants a divorce. We can't

git along together nohow. It's lonesome enough fer to live in the mountains when a man an' a woman keers for one another. But when she's a-spittin' like a wildcat or a-sullenin' like a hoot-owl, a man ain't got no call to live with her.

"There she be—a-talkin' like all git-out. Jes' listen to them names she calls me. So I'm a no-count vermint a-layin' on my back with a jug of corn whiskey, am I?

"Listen here, Justice. She—she keeps a-throwin' skillet lids, an' slings bilin' water on the best coondog in the Cumberlands, an' sets herself agin cookin' a man's victuals, an' then she—

"There, ya see. A man cain't hush her up nohow. Well, I spect ya heared a-plenty. What kin ya do about gittin' us out o' this pesky fix?

"You say we kin get a divorce? That be what I am a-hankerin' after. How much it cost—fer this divorce? Five dollars! That be a pow'ful heap o' money, but reckon it all be worth a heap more. Lucky I sold a bearskin an' two foxes. I got five dollars right here—in this tobacci bag. There ya be. Now jes' give me that paper, an' I—

"Hush ya mouth, Ariela! Ya cain't talk like that to me nohow. What ya mean, 'tain't settled? Here's the paper. Ya cain't call me names no more.

"What ya mean—ali-money? What be that? Oh. So I got to pay ya fer a-goin' ter your brother Ed, up on Hogback Mountain, do I? An' ya want to buy shoes an' snuff, do ya? Well, I jes' ain't a-goin' ter do it.

"What's that, Justice? If I don' pay I be in contempt of co't. But five dollars—fer ali-money. I never 'spect to be a-payin' fer that. Anyhow I ain't got no more money. I done paid ya all I had—fer that divorce.

"Well, if ya gimme till tomorrow, I might be able to scrape it up.

"Come on, Areila, we might as well git down to Uncle Ziah's fer the night."

It was dark when Benaja Widdup walked home for supper that evening. The figure of a man with his hat pulled down low, accosted him with a rifle and demanded his money. The justice replied he had only a five-dollar bill. The robber insisted that Benaja roll it up and stick it in the barrel of his rifle.

The next afternoon the couple returned to the office. In the presence of the justice, Ransie handed to his wife a five-dollar bill. It was curled up as if it had been rolled and inserted in the end of a gun-barrel. But the justice made no comment about it and fulfilled his duty by presenting to each a decree of divorce.

The couple stood in awkward silence. Then Ransie spoke almost sadly to his former wife.

"Well, I—I guess I be goin' back to the cabin. An' you air goin' to yer brother, Ed.

"What ya say, Ariela? Naw, I won't forgit—the bread in the tin box a-settin' on the shelf, an' the bacon in the bilin' pot. An' I won't forgit to wind the clock. Well, I better be a-goin'.

"Sure, Ariela, I'll be a-sayin' good-by to ya. I'd be a hound dog not to. 'Spect that's right. It will be mighty lonesome in the old cabin without ya. But when folks git mad an' wants a divorce—

" 'Tain't so. Ya wanted the pesky divorce as much as I did. Ya didn'? Well, then why didn' ya holler out an' say so?

"Ariela, ya look so—so sad—like them eyes of our coon-dog. An' ya talk real soft—like the way ya done when I first git sweet on ya.

"I reckon I bin mean an'— What ya say? Ya won't git mad at me no more? Well, come on then. We kin git home by sundown if—

"Why—what's the matter, Justice? We don' need yer advice no more. Not so fast, them air mighty big words. What ya mean—we is defyin' the laws o' Tennessee? I paid ya five dollars, ain't I? Huh? We air no longer man an' wife? Yep, we got a divorce, but— Oh. Well, then take this paper back an' we git no divorce.

"Come along, Ariela, let's git goin'.

"Aw, Justice, cain't ya let us be? We done change our mind. We a-goin' back to our cabin. Sure, I'm a law-abidin' man. I don' want to go agin what's right. What kin we do? Mattermoney? Why, Justice, we did all that a long time ago. Ya mean I am single now—like I was afore I git married? An' Ariela, she be single too? Whee. That happened pow'ful quick.

"Well, I reckon ya know the law, so go ahead. But how much it cost fer this—er—mattermoney? Five dollars. But Justice, I ain't got no more money. I done paid you all I had.

"Ariela, what ya a-doin' with that five dollars? That be yer ali-money. But ya be wantin' to buy shoes, snuff, an' things with that. So ya be a-willin' ter a-marryin' me agin? Ariela, I—I jes' cain't figger ya out. Yep, guess I be a-willin' to do it again. An' I promise never to be a-callin' ya a wildcat nohow.

"All right, Justice, reckon we be ready to listen to that—er—mattermoney talk, if you be."

DELLA YOUNG

From *The Gift of the Magi*

O. Henry lived in New York during the early 1900's and fell in love with "Bagdad-on-the-Subway" as he called that city. Many of his stories take place in humble, eight-dollars-per-week flats.

In such a scene we meet Della and James Dillingham Young. They are a devoted couple married just a year or so. It is the day before Christmas, but no joyful anticipation of it is in Della's heart. Let her explain why.

Three times I counted the heap of coins spilled on the kitchen table. But the total was always the same. One dollar and eighty-seven cents. That was all I had to buy a Christmas present for Jim. It made me sad. Sad enough to sniffle and cry. And I did.

I didn't want to buy anything ordinary—like a necktie—or a pair of gloves—even though he didn't own a pair of them. What I wanted was something worthy of Jim—something unusual—even rare, perhaps. I whiled away many a happy hour pretending that I was buying a wonderful gift for him. But then

I'd count the money again. It still added up the same. I had another cry.

I tried to convince myself that Jim would be grateful for any simple present. What counted most was our love for each other. And we were proud about something else. For Jim, it was a gold watch. It had belonged to his father, and before that to his grandfather. Of the few things Jim owned, that watch meant more to him than anything else.

What I was proud about was my hair. It does sound vain to admit it. Jim admired it too, and would say fancy-like—that it was "a cascade of brown water"—when I loosened it and it fell below my knees.

As I paced nervously about the room on this morning before Christmas, I caught a reflection of myself in the mirror. I glanced at my hair which I always arranged with care. I gasped as a sudden idea came to me. For a moment I hesitated—then I hurriedly put on my old brown coat and shabby brown hat.

A few minutes later I stood in front of a shop and read the sign: Madame Sofroni. Hair Goods of All Kinds.

I ran up one flight of stairs and opened a door. A large woman asked what I wished.

"Will you buy my hair?" I panted.

She asked me to take off my hat and undo my hair. She examined it and agreed to give me twenty dollars.

"Do it quickly," I said, trying to hold back some tears. It took no time at all until every strand was snipped off.

Then for the next two hours I had a dandy time looking around the stores for a present for Jim. And then I found it. It was made for Jim and no one else. I hadn't seen anything like it in any of the other stores. But here it was—a platinum fob. It wasn't flashy—had a simple design—which fine things always have. It would look so handsome on Jim's watch. So much better than the old leather strap which he used instead of a chain. I asked the price and held my breath. It was twenty-one dollars. I could buy it. I was so happy as I hurried home, and hugged my purse with the fob and eighty-seven cents in it.

When I got back to our flat, I bravely faced the mirror. Something had to be done to pretty my hair—what was left of it. So I got out the curling iron, lighted the gas, and did my best. Forty minutes later my head was covered with tiny curls.

What would Jim say when he saw me? He would kill me before he took a second look. He'd probably say that I looked like a Coney Island chorus girl.

By seven o'clock that evening the coffee was made, the frying pan was on the back of the stove ready to cook the chops. Jim was never late. I held the fob chain in my hand and sat near the door. Then I heard his steps on the stairs away down on the first flight. I whispered a little prayer: *Please God, make him think I am still pretty.*

The smile faded from Jim's face as he stared at me with a peculiar expression.

"Jim, dear. Please don't look at me that way. I had my hair cut. I sold it because—well—I couldn't let Christmas come without giving you a present. It'll grow out again. I just had to do it . Say 'Merry Christmas,' Jim, and let's be happy.

"Yes, Jim, it's gone. I sold it. Don't you like me just as well, anyhow? I'm me without my hair, ain't I?"

"You needn't look around for it, Jim. It ain't here. Anyhow I can't paste it back on. It's sold. Please don't be angry, dear. It's Christmas Eve. Maybe the hairs of my head were numbered, but nobody could ever count my love for you.

"Thanks for saying that, Jim—that you still love me—even with a haircut. Shall I put the chops on?"

Then Jim drew a package from his overcoat pocket and threw it on the table.

"What's that, Jim? Your present for me? Oh, thank you, dear. I can hardly wait to see what it is."

I quickly opened the package. "Oh, Jim, they're beautiful! You remembered—when we saw these combs in that store window on Broadway. The sign said—Pure tortoise shell with jeweled rims. And here I am holding them. I'll feel like a fashionable Fifth

Avenue lady wearing these combs. Of course I can't do it by tomorrow. But my hair grows so fast. You'll see."

I hugged and kissed him. I was touched by his generosity for I knew the combs were expensive. It was now time to give my present.

"Oh, I almost forgot yours. Here you are, dear."

Jim looked at the fob in his hand but remained silent.

"Ain't it dandy? I hunted all over town to find it. Now you'll have to look at the time a hundred times a day. Give me your watch, dear. I want to see how lovely it'll look.

"What's the matter, dear? Don't you like it? You did what? Oh, Jim, how could you! So you sold your beautiful watch to buy my combs. You did all that —for me."

I tried to smile and blink back my tears as I fumbled for my handkerchief.

"All right, Jim, let's do that. Let's put our Christmas presents away for awhile. They're too—too lovely to use right now.

"All right, dear. I'll put the chops on."

About The Author

Clay Franklin can be considered an authority in the specialized dramatic form known as the monologue. I STEP FROM A FAMOUS STORY is his fifth volume of such entertainment. They have won approval from such diversified sources as the press, stage and television personalities, and teachers of drama.

As solo actor, he has presented a program of character sketches, *Peeps at People*, before various groups.

Several three-act plays are under his authorship, also a number of short stories. As a director, Mr. Franklin has been associated with numerous productions for recognized community and summer theatres.

SAMUELFRENCH.COM

THE TWO OF US
Michael Frayn

Black and Silver
1m, 1f / Interior

In this scene, parents are awakened in the night by the baby. They stumble about trying to pacify the infant. At one point the husband panics because he cannot hear the baby breathing in the cradle, which is only reasonable because the wife has put it on their bed.

The New Quixote
1m, 1f / Interior

A woman on the verge of middle age spent the night in her flat with a 20 year old she met at a party. Now it's Sunday morning, and the boy returns with all his records and books. He announces that he has found happiness and intends to stay. He is so sincere that she is swept along in the tide of his new found love.

Mr. Foot
Comedy / 1m, 1f / Interior

It seems the man's foot jiggles uncontrollably at various moments and the woman enjoys discussing this with a little man who isn't there.

Chinamen
Farce / 1m, 1f / Interior

Two actors play five characters. She has asked a woman, her new hippy boyfriend and some other guests for dinner. He invited the woman's deserted husband. The object is to keep the estranged husband and wife apart. They dine in two different rooms and maneuver the guests so that these two are never in the same room.

BLUE YONDER
Kate Aspengren

Dramatic Comedy / Monolgues and scenes
12f (can be performed with as few as 4 with doubling) / Unit Set

A familiar adage states, "Men may work from sun to sun, but women's work is never done." In Blue Yonder, the audience meets twelve mesmerizing and eccentric women including a flight instructor, a firefighter, a stuntwoman, a woman who donates body parts, an employment counselor, a professional softball player, a surgical nurse professional baseball player, and a daredevil who plays with dynamite among others. Through the monologues, each woman examines her life's work and explores the career that she has found. Or that has found her.

www.ingramcontent.com/pod-product-compliance
Lightning Source LLC
Chambersburg PA
CBHW070643300426
44111CB00013B/2242